Exposing the Myths

The Realities of Abortion Practices

by

Dr. ant

Exposing the Myths: The Realities of Abortion Practices

Contents

Introduction

In the kaleidoscope of human narratives, there lies a singularly potent story laced with profound moral, societal, and personal threads—abortion. As we stand at the crossroads of complex realities, it's imperative to unravel the multifaceted layers that conceal the truths of this sensitive subject. This introduction serves as a beacon to delve deep into a subject that touches the conscience of civilizations and reverberates through the corridors of both history and hearts.

The abortion debate isn't just an intellectual confrontation but an emotional tempest that has swelled, ebbed, and evolved over centuries. It encapsulates not just a clash of ideologies but a profound human drama that binds individuals to the core challenges of existence, inviting profound ethical reflections. How does one reconcile the sanctity of life with the autonomy of choice? This question has engendered passionate discourse and shapes the mosaic of discussions presented in this book.

For Roman Catholics, whose faith draws upon the timeless teachings and moral philosophies derived from scripture and tradition, abortion occupies a fraught yet clear position. It's seen as not just a medical or societal issue but an affront to the deeper spiritual convictions held sacrosanct. The sanctity of life, as delineated within Catholic doctrine, provides the moral compass guiding adherents through the murky waters of modern debates.

Historians, too, find the contours of abortion debates trenchant with lessons from the past, helping unveil how cultural, legal, and scientific evolutions shape our current perspectives. They map out the trajectory of this practice from antiquity through its concealment and emergence in varying social contexts. Abortion reflects societal mores, governments' roles, and the perennial struggle between progress and ethical integrity, making it a mirror through which to glimpse human tendencies across epochs.

For pregnant mothers, the issue is personal and corporeal, far beyond philosophical flights. It navigates the deeply personal valleys of fear, hope, and the myriad challenges pregnancy can entail. The physical and emotional journey associated with pregnancy stitches a tapestry of anxiety and expectation, often influenced by the societal narratives that swirl around them.

This book aims to explore and expose the realities of abortion, focusing on its profound impact on women, families, and society. It challenges the cloaked lies perpetuated by what can often be described as an unscrupulous industry. Through careful analysis and narrative discourse, we aim to strip back the façades and reveal the devastating consequences that ripple outwards from the act and the ideology of abortion itself.

In adopting the stylistic hues inspired by past philosophical and theological giants, this book sees the subject not just as a mere transaction but a philosophical battleground. The narrative echoes of Saint Thomas Aquinas' reasoned articulations and G.K. Chesterton's probing parables—where logic meets creativity in robust dialogue—invite readers into an immersive exploration. And with an eye toward the comprehensive perspective akin to that of Pope Saint John Paul II, we seek not just theoretical understanding but holistic engagement.

The larger tapestry of chapters explores the myriad subcultures of this challenging topic—examining the practices, the historical shifts in viewpoints, and the diverging cultural landscapes. This introductory discourse thus serves as both a preface and a promise to offer balanced insights into a global phenomenon of significant consequence. We'll traverse painful truths, bittersweet stories, and maybe even find redemption paths.

Yet, as we examine these multifarious aspects, it remains crucial to remember the human elements at the heart of these narratives—the women, the unborn, the families, and the communities impacted. Empathy, understanding, and truth must guide us as we tread these often-contentious pathways.

Through nuanced discussions in each chapter, we endeavor to construct an informed narrative—a tapestry woven from facts, ethical considerations, and the personal journeys of those affected. We'll ask tough questions, challenge prevailing myths, and dissect the fabric of societal norms that have shaped the abortion landscape as we know it.

As you delve deeper into the pages that follow, reflecting on legal perspectives, medical insights, ethical principles, and cultural contexts, our ambition is that this exploration will not just illuminate but inspire— spurring thoughtful reflection, fostering compassion, and perhaps culminating in a transformative understanding of what it means to uphold the dignity of life amidst the swirling tides of choice and consequence.

The journey through this book may position one's perspective, deepen personal convictions, or even challenge preconceived notions, but the ultimate journey must be to the heart—a quest toward healing, truth, and a future tinged with hope driven by justice and love for all stages of life.

Chapter 1: The Overview of Abortion Practices

The history of abortion practices is a complex tapestry woven through centuries, reflecting shifts in societal values and advances in technology. As the methods have evolved, so too have the legal and cultural frameworks that envelop them, crafting a story fraught with moral dilemmas and ethical debates. This topic can't simply be confined to the realm of individual choice; it reverberates through every fiber of society, touching the core of human relationships and echoing in the corridors of family and community life. In understanding the overview of abortion practices, we unspool a narrative that speaks not only to a medical procedure but also to the profound impact it wields on women, families, and the larger societal fabric. The interplay between cultural acceptance and legislative action forms a battle that is as much about the heart as it is about the law, challenging us to question the truths we hold dear and the consequences we perpetuate. As this chapter unfolds, we will journey through a landscape that juxtaposes hope and despair, highlighting the urgent need for a renewed examination of the values that steer our collective path.

The Evolution of Abortion Methods

Abortion methods have transformed considerably over the centuries, shaped by medical advancements, societal attitudes, and ethical debates. As we've journeyed through time, these changes reflect humanity's evolving understanding of life, health, and morality. Just as with any significant shift in societal practices, the evolution of abortion methods tells us much about the worldviews and priorities of different eras.

In ancient times, abortion methods were often rudimentary and perilous. Without the scope of modern medicine, women faced grave risks when attempting to terminate a pregnancy. Herbal concoctions, many of which were more toxic than effective, were among the earliest methods. Women would consume various plants or substances believed to induce miscarriage, though success was inconsistent at best. Some records from ancient Greece and Rome suggest the use of sharp instruments, but these methods were dangerous, often leading to severe injury or death.

The Middle Ages did not see significant advancement in abortion methods. Instead, cultural and religious influences shaped the practice. As Christianity's reach extended across Europe, religious doctrine began to play a vital role in shaping attitudes toward abortion. The Church's strong opposition meant that abortion, when practiced, was done clandestinely, with methods varying drastically in safety and efficacy. Women who sought to terminate pregnancies often turned to clandestine practitioners, with outcomes as uncertain as in antiquity.

The Renaissance and Enlightenment brought new attitudes towards science and medicine. As anatomists and physicians began to understand the human body better, more sophisticated – and marginally safer – methods began to emerge. Surgical techniques, albeit crude by today's standards, began to develop. However, these methods remained risky, and the stigma surrounding abortion meant that such procedures were often performed in secrecy.

Moving into the 19th century, the Industrial Revolution spurred advancements in medical technology and practices. The public health movement and the rise of modern medical ethics began to influence how abortions were performed and perceived. Yet, this era was also marked by legal restrictions that criminalized abortion in many parts of the world. As a result, the practice continued underground, with midwives or unqualified practitioners often administering care. The methods remained fraught with danger, and mortality rates were high.

It wasn't until the 20th century that abortion methods underwent significant transformation, mainly due to breakthroughs in medical science. The introduction of antiseptics and anesthesia revolutionized surgical procedures, including those for terminating pregnancies. Vaccines and antibiotics reduced the risks of infections, making surgical methods safer and more reliable. The mid-20th century saw the development of vacuum aspiration and dilation and curettage (D&C), which became the standard surgical techniques for abortions. These developments promised improved safety and outcomes for women seeking abortions.

Parallel to surgical advancements, the late 20th century witnessed the emergence of medical abortions. The introduction of medications like RU-486 (also known as mifepristone) changed the landscape fundamentally, offering a non-invasive alternative to surgical procedures. These medical methods allowed for earlier termination of pregnancies with fewer complications, symbolizing a shift in how abortions could be managed.

Today, with both surgical and medical options available, abortion methods are more diverse and, for the most part, much safer than in previous centuries. However, the evolution of these methods is not just a tale of medical progress. It also highlights the persisting ethical and moral dilemmas faced by societies worldwide. As science and technology continue to advance, so too will the ways we address the complex issues surrounding abortion.

In reflecting on this evolution, one can't ignore the societal and cultural narratives that have both constrained and propelled these changes. The tension between personal autonomy, societal norms, and ethical considerations continues to shape the methods and accessibility of abortion worldwide. While some argue these advancements empower women with choices that were previously unavailable, others contend that they contribute to a broader devaluation of human life.

The modern era presents its own set of challenges and debates. As the debates around reproductive rights intensify, technological advancements such as telemedicine have introduced new dimensions. They make access possible in regions where in-person services are restricted, further transforming the landscape of abortion care. Yet, these advancements prompt discourse around the implications of technology in healthcare, highlighting the age-old struggle between progress and morality.

The story of abortion methods is a reflection of human society itself, mirroring its strengths, weaknesses, beliefs, and contradictions. It serves as a reminder of how deeply intertwined technological advances are with the moral compass of society. As we look to the future, the evolution of these methods will undoubtedly continue, influenced by ongoing ethical discussions and technological innovations. How societies choose to reconcile these developments with their values remains an open question, one that will likely resonate for generations to come.

Legal and Cultural Perspectives on Abortion

The conversation around abortion is as much entrenched in the corridors of law as it is in the cultural fabric of society. To understand the legal frameworks, one must first grasp the diverse cultural perspectives that shape them. The laws that govern abortion reflect closely held beliefs, ranging from its perceived morality to its social ramifications. These perspectives are not static; they evolve alongside shifts in societal norms and cultural understanding.

Culturally, abortion has always been a polarizing topic, deeply rooted in values that can vary not just from country to country, but within communities. In many societies, the sanctity of life is a core tenet that guides actions and beliefs, a principle that finds resonance in Roman Catholic doctrine. For many believers, life is sacred from conception, a gift worthy of protection against all worldly impositions. This view elevates the status of the unborn child to that of a living person, bestowed with rights and dignity. The cultural touchstone for such perspectives is the family unit, which is often seen as a microcosm of society and a sanctuary for human life.

On the legal front, the intersection of culture and jurisprudence presents a complex tapestry. Some legal systems have embraced a liberal stance, enshrining a woman's right to choose in the name of autonomy and privacy. Others have laid down stringent restrictions, grounded in moral arguments about preserving life. The way laws are structured can often be a reflection of the predominant cultural attitudes within a nation; it's both a race and a ballet, fluid and sometimes reactionary, where morality dances with autonomy on the legislative stage.

In democratic societies, the legal perspectives on abortion are frequently the heart of fervent debates. Legislation often oscillates between ensuring women's rights and protecting potential life, influenced by advocacy from both pro-life and pro-choice movements. Each legal challenge or reform encounters vehement arguments, as constituents hold tightly onto their cultural mores and ethical convictions. This dichotomy is particularly evident in the United States, where landmark cases like Roe v. Wade have incited decades of discourse and legislative tug-of-war.

Meanwhile, cultural perspectives on abortion can shape the societal acceptance or rejection of legal verdicts. In nations where cultural norms fiercely oppose abortion, the laws might reflect strict anti-abortion sentiments. For others, cultural shifts could usher in progressive reforms, allowing for broader access and rights. The cultural milieu becomes a sieve through which legal impositions either gain social support or face vigorous opposition.

Across the globe, the influence of religion, tradition, and socioeconomic factors can produce a broad spectrum of attitudes. In countries where Catholicism is predominant, such as Ireland historically, there has been significant resistance to liberalizing abortion laws, although recent reforms indicate changing tides influenced by cultural shifts. Here, religion often casts a long shadow over legal frameworks, intertwining faith and governance into a complex weave that shapes societal norms.

These cultural perspectives aren't merely confined to national boundaries but can be contrasted around the world. In regions where individual freedom and modernity hold sway, laws may be more permissive. However, even within such areas, cultural pockets may retain conservative views, creating an intricate mosaic of attitudes within a single jurisdiction.

The struggle between legal stipulations and cultural beliefs often results in societal tension, manifesting in public demonstrations, legal battles, and advocacy campaigns. The discourse is not limited to policymakers; it filters down to ordinary lives, affecting personal decisions and family dynamics. The fear of societal judgment or legal repercussions can weigh heavily on individuals confronted with abortion decisions, demonstrating the profound interplay of legality and culture on personal experiences.

A significant cultural consideration in this debate is the notion of choice versus duty. Modern narratives often frame the discussion around choice — a woman's right to decide what happens to her body. Yet, in stark contrast, other's cultural teachings emphasize communal duty and responsibility. For communities steeped in extended family structures, the decision about abortion extends beyond the individual, involving families and community opinions, thereby intertwining personal choices with collective morality.

Legal and cultural perspectives on abortion are also reflections of historical trends. Over centuries, abortion practices and attitudes have evolved, often reverting to ancient philosophies during times of societal upheaval or reform. Historically, abortion rights have cycled through periods of liberalization and restriction, reflecting the ebbs and flows of cultural readiness to embrace or reject these freedoms. The past is a mirror where one can observe the reframing of laws and cultural beliefs, a continuum upon which current debates stand.

In navigating these turbulent waters, it becomes crucial to engage with both legal principles and cultural ethics to glean a holistic understanding of where society stands on abortion. The legal frameworks surrounding abortion are as diverse as cultural attitudes, and neither exists in a vacuum. For historians, pregnant mothers, and faithful Catholics alike, understanding this interplay sheds light on the profound impacts these perspectives have on individual lives and broader societal constructs.

Ultimately, the legal and cultural perspectives on abortion are testament to the ongoing negotiation between personal morality and collective legislation, a dance of values that defines the ethos of any society. Amidst this backdrop, one cannot ignore the solemn weight of truth and the burden of decision that women bear in such a legal and cultural landscape. As future legislation arises and cultural attitudes continue to evolve, the dialogue between the law and societal mores will undoubtedly persevere, compelling us to question and define the kind of world we aspire to create.

Chapter 2: Surgical Abortion Techniques

In the somber corridors of modern medicine, where ethics intertwine uncomfortably with advancements, surgical abortion techniques evoke a profound moral debate that can't be easily dismissed. These procedures, often shrouded in clinical jargon, lay bare the stark reality of invasive interventions like dilation and evacuation or suction aspiration. Such methods, touted as necessary by some, unravel the delicate tapestry of life with cold precision. Yet, beneath the sterile veil, these techniques reveal a dystopian underbelly that testifies to a deeper societal malaise. By confronting these surgical practices, we are drawn into a narrative that challenges not just medical ethics, but the very essence of our collective humanity. It's here that the soul searches for answers amid the dissonance of technological prowess and the unmistakable fragility of life—a dialogue that beckons history, theology, and conscience to the forefront of this essential human conversation.

Analysis of Dilation and Evacuation

The technique known as Dilation and Evacuation (D&E) is a complex procedure often performed during the second trimester of pregnancy, typically between 13 to 24 weeks. Within the context of surgical abortion methods, D&E stands as one of the most contentious and scrutinized techniques due to its nature and implications. Historically, the second trimester has been a period fraught with moral and medical debates, reflecting the tension between advancing medical science and the intrinsic value of nascent human life.

From a clinical perspective, D&E is usually recommended in cases where the pregnancy poses significant health risks to the mother, or when severe fetal anomalies are detected. This procedure consists of two main components: the dilation of the cervix to allow for the passage and removal of fetal tissue, and the evacuation, which involves the use of surgical instruments like forceps and curettes to remove the fetus. The precision required and the emotional weight borne by practitioners underscore the profound ethical dilemmas embedded within such interventions.

In the realm of Catholic ethics, a domain deeply skeptical of modern abortion techniques, D&E represents more than a medical procedure—it embodies a moral crossroad. The act of terminating a pregnancy after the first trimester heightens the clash between medical needs and the Catholic conception of the inviolable sanctity of life. This perspective is echoed throughout the Church's teachings, advocating for the protection of life from conception until natural death, and viewing abortion as a profound violation of divine law.

The narratives surrounding D&E are often laden with distress and sorrow, not only affecting mothers but entire families, as these stories are woven into the fabric of community and personal histories. The emotional impact is not limited to the patients but extends to healthcare professionals, who may experience moral injury or conflict. The decision-making process in opting for this procedure is rarely uncomplicated, burdened with layers of ethical considerations and societal judgments.

In examining D&E, it is crucial to interrogate the societal narratives that influence perceptions of necessary medical interventions versus elective choices. The societal discourse often morphs the clinical reality into a moral battleground, where one's stance on such procedures might be seen as a reflection of their character or morality. This dichotomy fuels a larger debate about the nature of human rights, bodily autonomy, and the ethical responsibilities of modern medicine.

Through a utopian lens, one might envision a world where the circumstances leading to D&E are rare, brought forth by a profound respect for the dignity of life, accessible healthcare, and genuine support systems for pregnant individuals. In this ideal setting, advances in neonatal care and preventive health could reduce the necessity of such procedures, shifting the focus towards nurturing life in all its stages. Conversely, a dystopian view might lament the current societal state, highlighting the way such procedures have become emblematic of broader moral and ethical erosions.

Understanding the profound complexity of D&E requires a multifaceted exploration of continuing advancements in both medical practices and ethical frameworks. It forces us to ask uncomfortable yet essential questions about our collective values and the kind of society we strive to nurture. Is the reliance on procedures like D&E a testament to our scientific progress, or does it signal a deeper, systemic failure to uphold and cherish human life at all stages?

As historians unfold the layers of abortion practices across ages, the evolution witnessed in surgical methods like D&E holds a mirror to societal attitudes. It's a reflection not only of technological advancement but of varying degrees of moral flexibility and resistance within human society. Yet, amid such reflection, the steadfast principle for many remains—life is sacred, and its interruption, particularly through surgical means, is profoundly tragic.

In the end, the discussion of D&E isn't merely a clinical report or an ethical conundrum; it is a testament to humanity's ongoing struggle to reconcile our extraordinary capacity for scientific innovation with the equally boundless resource of compassion and morality. It invites dialogue not only amongst those within the valiant halls of medicine and ethics but across society at large, laying bare the collective conscience's raw edges as it grapples with the potent reality of life and its fragility.

Impact of Suction Aspiration

Suction aspiration, often referred to as vacuum aspiration, has become one of the most prevalent methods of surgical abortion in modern times. Its use underscores a controversial intersection of medical practice and societal ethics, sparking debates about the sanctity of life and the moral compass of our communities. As we delve deeper into the particulars of suction aspiration, a broader narrative unfolds, one that challenges us to question the humaneness and implications of this technique.

At its core, suction aspiration involves the insertion of a hollow tube through the cervix, connected to a powerful vacuum device which evacuates the contents of the uterus. This procedure, emerging prominently in the latter half of the 20th century, was hailed for its efficiency and quick recovery time. For many proponents, it promised a technical triumph in reproductive healthcare, offering a supposedly "safer" alternative to more invasive surgical methods. Yet, such clinical descriptions belie the profound moral and societal questions it raises.

For Roman Catholics, the intrinsic value of life from conception cannot be understated. The sanctity accorded to the unborn is a principle deeply embedded in their faith. Suction aspiration, in this context, not only terminates a potential life but also confronts core beliefs about human dignity and divine creation. It presents a dystopian vision where the miracle of life is reduced to a clinical procedure, raising somber questions about humanity's stewardship over life and death.

Moreover, historians looking back at the evolving narrative of abortion methods may note suction aspiration as a significant turning point. It's a technique that reflects advancements in medical technology but also an unsettling shift in society's comfort with terminating pregnancies. Where once there was ambiguity and clandestine practices, now stands a sterile, efficient process that strips away previous barriers and moral qualms for some. This shift speaks to a broader cultural and ethical transformation that historians will continue to analyze for its societal impacts.

For pregnant mothers, the impact of suction aspiration extends beyond immediate physical outcomes. Many women are left grappling with emotional and psychological effects that are often minimized in discourse surrounding abortion. Despite being portrayed as a straightforward procedure, the reality for many includes feelings of loss, regret, and sorrow. These are experiences that can't be quantified or easily dismissed, often requiring a robust support system to navigate the aftermath. Society's failure to acknowledge and address these repercussions further marginalizes those who undergo the procedure.

Medical professionals who perform suction aspiration are not immune to the moral dilemmas posed by the procedure. Faced with the ethical responsibility of patient care, they navigate the delicate balance between providing medical assistance and confronting the contentious nature of abortion. The procedure, though seen as technically simple within medical circles, carries with it a heavy ethical and emotional weight. This weight is borne not just by the individuals directly involved, but by the wider community as it reflects on the definition of progress and morality.

The suction aspiration technique underscores a much larger societal conversation about the direction of modern healthcare and the ethics intertwined with it. As we grapple with these issues, it is critical that we approach them with sensitivity, respect, and a commitment to understanding the multifaceted dimensions of human life. The decisions made within clinical settings ripple outward, affecting societal values, family dynamics, and community health.

In a utopian society, every individual would hold an unwavering respect for life at all stages, recognizing the sacredness of existence gifted by a higher power. Suction aspiration challenges us to envision such a world— a world where the sanctity of life is revered, and where compassion for both the unborn and the mothers is prioritized. This vision calls for a collective reflection on how technological advancements can coexist with ethical principles that honor life in all its forms.

Ultimately, the impact of suction aspiration is multifaceted and profound, resonating well beyond the sterile confines of a medical facility. It touches on timeless questions of morality, the essence of humanity, and the very fabric of societal values. By engaging with these questions earnestly and empathetically, we aim not only to understand the procedure's implications but to seek a path forward that upholds the dignity of all involved.

Chapter 3: Medical Abortion Procedures

In the quiet corridors of uncertainty, medical abortion procedures, often seen as a modern alternative to surgical methods, present their own array of dystopian realities wrapped in promises of ease. Rooted in chemical interactions, these procedures primarily involve the use of drugs like mifepristone (RU-486) and methotrexate to end early pregnancies. Yet, beneath the clinical terms and perceived convenience lies a complex web of physical and emotional upheaval. While advocates tout medical abortions as non-invasive, they seldom discuss the sometimes severe side effects and potential health risks that trail behind. Historically forgotten in discussions are the profound impacts on women's mental well-being and the ripple effects on families and society. The narrative woven around these methods frequently obscures the underlying moral dilemmas and societal costs, leaving behind questions of ethics as stark reminders of the chasm between technological advancement and humane care.

Understanding RU-486

The advent of RU-486, or mifepristone, marked a turning point in the realm of medical abortion procedures. Developed in the late 20th century, this drug offered a new method for terminating pregnancies that didn't involve surgical intervention. Initially hailed as a scientific breakthrough, RU-486 quickly became the subject of intense debate, transcending medical circles to dominate ethical and religious discussions around the globe. It promised autonomy and simplicity, but not without a significant moral cost that must be understood. In the context of our duty to defend the sanctity of life, RU-486 presents a dystopian vision of medical convenience overshadowing moral values.

The mechanism of RU-486 works with remarkable, if chilling, efficacy. Mifepristone functions by blocking progesterone, a hormone crucial for maintaining pregnancy. Without progesterone, the uterine lining breaks down, leading to the detachment of the embryo. This process is augmented by a subsequent drug, misoprostol, which induces contractions to expel the pregnancy. What appears merely as a series of calculated biochemical interactions in a lab setting belies the profound ethical implications and the emotional turmoil it inflicts on countless women.

Proponents of RU-486 argue its effectiveness and non-invasive nature as significant advancements in reproductive health. However, they often overlook the deep psychological impact and societal ramifications embedded within these pills. In a world striving for utopian ideals, where every person is ensured dignity and moral agency, the promotion of RU-486 as a straightforward solution to unwanted pregnancies raises troubling questions. Are we diminishing the intrinsic value of life by reducing it to a matter of medical convenience? Can such a profound decision be ethically reconciled with a pill?

Lean into the societal narrative surrounding RU-486, and you'll encounter a disturbing paradox. It stands as a supposed beacon of female empowerment, yet reinforces a culture that often devalues life at its most vulnerable stage. The cultural acceptance of RU-486 might seem like progress to some, yet it reflects a utilitarian mindset that disregards the nuanced understanding of human dignity. As followers of faith and tradition, we must scrutinize the moral and ethical underpinnings that support such solutions.

Throughout history, great minds have debated the nature of human life and our responsibility to protect it. In this context, RU-486 challenges longstanding moral frameworks and compels us to revisit foundational ethical principles. Can modern society maintain its humanity while embracing such practices? We must consider whether the reliance on pills like RU-486 aligns with a genuine care for women and families or merely serves to mask deeper societal issues, such as lack of support for expectant mothers.

One of the most unsettling aspects of RU-486 is how its purported ease of use can obscure the potential trauma faced by women who undertake medical abortions. Unlike surgical procedures performed in medical settings under professional supervision, RU-486 transfers the experience to the lone confines of a woman's home. It demands that she confront not only the physical manifestations of the abortion but also the potential emotional and psychological consequences. Can we, in good conscience, overlook these impacts as merely collateral? Society should not forsake its duty of care and compassion for the sake of expedience.

The realities of RU-486 present a grim reflection on how society addresses unplanned pregnancies. Underneath the statistics and clinical outcomes lies the broken narrative of lives touched by anguish, regret, and a longing for something more substantial than fleeting solutions. In a truly compassionate society, alternatives that respect both the life of the unborn and the wellbeing of the mother should be the priority. The simplicity of popping a pill shouldn't cloud our vision or pave the way for neglecting comprehensive care and support systems.

As with any medical intervention, RU-486 is not without its risks. While not the focus herein, it's essential to acknowledge that these risks aren't just physical but span the emotional spectrum as well. It's imperative to question whether we're genuinely supporting women or inadvertently encouraging a form of medical alienation. Are these decisions made with informed consent and genuine understanding, or are they dictated by fleeting societal norms and pressures?

The challenge for Catholics, historians, and all those invested in the sanctity of life is to illuminate the profound and enduring truth that each life is a gift, imbued with purpose and divine value. RU-486, emblematic of a broader cultural shift, urges us to reconsider what genuine progress looks like. It's a stark reminder that while science may offer new possibilities, it doesn't absolve the moral responsibility that remains.

In pondering the implications of RU-486, the task before us is to forge a future not defined merely by technological capabilities but enriched by moral clarity and compassionate understanding. As stewards of life, our duty is to cultivate a culture that cherishes each stage of existence, affirming the hopeful utopian vision where all lives are valued and protected.

Side Effects and Risks of Methotrexate

In the annals of medical abortion procedures, methotrexate stands as a pharmacological warrior against unwanted pregnancy. Yet, like any warrior, it carries with it the scars and burdens of its battles. While it serves a purpose, the side effects and potential complications of methotrexate reveal a reality that should not be obscured by the clamor of modern medical solutions.

Methotrexate, originally developed as a chemotherapy agent, works by inhibiting the rapid cell division that pregnancy necessitates. It is this very mechanism that knits together both its therapeutic utility and its potential for harm. By its action, it not only targets the cells of the developing embryo but also affects other rapidly dividing cells in a woman's body. This can lead to a range of side effects that vary in severity but invariably provide a tangible reminder of the drug's powerful reach.

Commonly, women undergoing methotrexate for medical abortion may experience gastrointestinal disturbances. This can manifest as nausea, vomiting, or diarrhea. The digestive system, with its own rapidly dividing cells, often bears early signs of the drug's indiscriminate nature. Some women describe it as akin to seasickness, a constant churning that parallels the emotional turmoil they may be experiencing.

More severe complications, although rarer, tell a grimmer tale. Methotrexate can provoke hepatic toxicity, with elevations in liver enzymes indicating stress or damage to the liver. This is particularly concerning given the organ's vital role in processing and filtering the very pharmaceutical agents consumed. In some cases, this toxicity can lead to liver fibrosis or even cirrhosis over time, painting a picture of chronic health decline rather than temporary relief.

Anemia is another risk, as methotrexate interferes with the bone marrow's ability to produce new blood cells. This can leave women feeling fatigued, light-headed, and generally weak—symptoms that are not easily reconciled with the demands of daily life. The irony is bitter: to end a nascent life, methotrexate diminishes the life force of the mother, even if temporarily.

Beyond the physical ramifications, methotrexate's psychological and emotional impact can be profound. The very act of undergoing a medical abortion can lead to a significant emotional toll. When compounded with a physical state that is anything but normal—accompanied by worry about potential long-term consequences—the mental journey becomes even more labyrinthine.

The procedural risks of methotrexate are also not to be underestimated. Healthcare providers try to mitigate this by closely monitoring the process, yet cases of incomplete abortion persist. This can result in the need for additional interventions, such as surgical evacuation, causing further physical and emotional strain on the woman involved.

It is also crucial to consider the social and familial landscapes that are often dramatically altered by the medical procedures that wield methotrexate as a tool. In this sphere, the effects can be as disruptive as a category five storm, sweeping away connections, leaving an emotional wasteland in its wake. The disconnect grows as those who are situated outside this sphere can't fully grasp the intricacies of the emotional and spiritual costs.

Methotrexate in medical abortion is not simply a matter of chemical reactions and physiological responses. Its use raises ethical and moral questions about the sanctity of life, the responsibility of healthcare providers, and the pervasive social attitudes towards pregnancy and motherhood. As it acts on the woman's body, altering it in noticeable ways, it also acts on society, posing challenges to what it means to nurture life and make choices about its continuance.

In a world that often offers complex technological and medical solutions, methotrexate serves as a reminder that consequences can be broader than anticipated. It's not just about the immediate effects on physical health but the long reverberations on the soul and society. The enduring impression is not just of a medical procedure but of an existential quandary, challenging us to question the paradigms through which we view life, health, and moral responsibility.

Chapter 4: The Birth Control Pill: Hidden Dangers

In our ongoing quest to unravel the truths often shielded by the facade of modern progress, we now turn our eyes to the birth control pill, a symbol of liberation yet a harbinger of unforeseen perils. Amidst glowing promises of freedom and empowerment, the little pill can impose silent chains of long-term health implications, lurking beneath its benign veneer. With each dose, the body quietly responds, not always with the harmony once envisioned. For Roman Catholics, historians, and mothers, the paradox grows apparent: the pill, heralded as a key to autonomy, shadows the sanctity of life itself by altering fundamental biological processes. Such disruption isn't merely physiological; it echoes through family and society, challenging our moral compass. One must ponder not only the physical ramifications but the societal metamorphosis it invites— a transformation that blurs the line between autonomy and the intrinsic value of life. Through this lens, we recognize how the pill, while wielding the banner of choice, often conceals a road paved with unforeseen consequences. The ramifications extend beyond individual freedom, asking us to reflect deeply on the intricate weave of life, health, and ethical duty.

How the Pill Works

In the tapestry of human life, the creation of life stands as a grand weaving of delicate threads, each necessary for the fulfillment of its intended beauty. The birth control pill, however, aims to sever these threads, controlling the natural order under the guise of empowerment. To truly understand its implications, we must delve into its intricate workings, painted in stark contrast to the harmonious symphony of life's creation.

The primary function of the birth control pill is to prevent ovulation. It achieves this by simulating the hormonal environment of pregnancy. By introducing synthetic hormones—estrogen and progestin—it tricks the body into believing conception is already underway. The body, in turn, halts the release of the egg as if safeguarding the nascent life it perceives to be growing.

This manipulation of the body's natural rhythms is no small feat. The synthetic hormones systematically suppress the pituitary gland's production of follicle-stimulating hormone (FSH) and luteinizing hormone (LH). In their absence, the development and release of eggs are halted—an illusion sustained on a delicate balance of chemical intervention. A single misstep in dosage can unravel it, bringing forth the very life it sought to prevent.

Beyond ovulation, the pill fortifies its mission with a two-pronged defensive strategy. First, it alters the cervical mucus, rendering it hostile to sperm. Thickening it into an impenetrable barrier, the pill ensures that even if an egg were to escape suppression, it would be challenging to encounter its counterpart. Secondly, it transforms the lining of the uterus. By making it inhospitable for a fertilized egg, it prevents the womb from becoming a cradle for new life.

These mechanisms paint a picture of cold efficiency, yet we must question the cost at which they operate. The pill acts not only upon the reproductive system but extends its influence across the body's entire hormonal ecosystem. Disruptions to this delicate balance can yield unforeseen repercussions, notably on a woman's emotional and physical well-being.

Despite its widespread acceptance, the pill's relationship with nature remains one of discord. In attempting to mold our biological reality, we risk severing the profound connection we maintain with the natural world. Therein lies a danger not just to individual women, but to society as a whole—disturbing the delicate dance between order and chaos that governs all life.

It is through this lens that one sees the pill's dual nature: both a liberator from unwanted burdens and a forceful denier of potential life. This dichotomy presents a moral and ethical dilemma, challenging us to reflect on the value we ascribe to the freedom of choice versus the sanctity of life.

At its core, the pill encourages us to reject a part of ourselves. The act of creation—intended to be joyful—is treated with skepticism, as if an enemy to be neutralized. It suggests a utopia where every consequence is manageable, where discretion can override destiny without fallout. And yet, stories of those who fare differently caution us against such optimism, illuminating the pitfalls of this modern convenience.

The ramifications of this choice echo beyond the reach of those who consume the pill. As societal norms shift, so does the philosophical understanding of life's beginning. The pill's silent approval alters perceptions, teaching the young that control equates to empowerment while quietly undermining the natural reverence for life's inception.

In sum, understanding how the pill works offers more than technical insight into its mechanisms—it opens a dialogue on the broader implications of altering nature and the possible dystopian future it beckons. It encourages us to reflect earnestly on the harmony we choose to disrupt in pursuit of personal agency, urging us to weigh our actions not only through the lens of individual convenience but through the spectrum of communal values and divine order.

Long-Term Health Implications

The introduction of the birth control pill marked a significant shift in reproductive health, offering women unprecedented control over their bodies. However, like many pharmaceutical advancements, it isn't without its hidden dangers, particularly when it comes to long-term health implications. With its seemingly innocuous presence, the pill conceals a complex web of potential side effects and health risks that can manifest over years or even decades.

At the heart of the issue lies the alteration of hormonal balance. The birth control pill works primarily by suppressing ovulation through the use of synthetic hormones. While this mechanism efficiently prevents pregnancy, it also disrupts the natural hormonal cycle, impacting various aspects of a woman's health over time. The body, designed to operate with its own intricate hormonal signals, can face challenges as it adjusts to synthetic hormone regulation.

One of the most debated health risks associated with long-term use of the pill is an increased susceptibility to certain types of cancer. Research has shown mixed outcomes, with some studies suggesting a decreased risk for ovarian and endometrial cancers yet an elevated risk for breast and cervical cancers. This dichotomy often leaves women caught in a difficult balancing act, where the benefits seem to come at an equally significant cost.

While cancer remains a leading concern, there is also considerable evidence linking birth control pills to cardiovascular issues. Long-term usage has been associated with a higher risk of blood clots, such as deep vein thrombosis and pulmonary embolism, especially in women who smoke or who have other underlying risk factors. The correlation between hormone-based contraceptives and stroke is similarly troubling, raising questions about the wider impact on women's cardiovascular health.

Equally concerning is the pill's influence on mental health. Hormonal fluctuations naturally affect mood and cognition, and the synthetic hormones in contraceptives can exacerbate these effects, potentially leading to depression or anxiety over prolonged periods. Many women might not immediately connect their mental health struggles to their continued use of the pill, attributing them instead to other life stressors, and thus, potential side effects remain unaddressed and untreated.

The disruption isn't confined to the physiological. The pill also subtly impacts lifestyle choices and societal roles. With the promise of liberated sexual freedom comes the unintended burden of responsibility for a woman's health resting mainly on her shoulders. This dynamic can alter personal relationships and societal expectations, steering women toward a path lined with decisions about managing side effects and health risks.

Moreover, the potential for long-term reproductive consequences cannot be ignored. Extended pill usage may contribute to difficulties in conception after cessation, as the body takes time to reestablish its natural hormonal rhythm. This scenario presents a paradox where a solution for preventing pregnancy could inadvertently complicate future family planning aspirations.

The way the pill metabolizes in the body also raises ecological and public health questions. Its by-products, often excreted into wastewater, join a growing list of pharmaceuticals found in water supplies, further complicating our relationship with synthetic hormone exposure beyond the individual level. Thus, the pill's long-term implications ripple outward, affecting broader environmental systems and human communities.

Further complicating these issues is the underrepresentation in research focused on the long-term impact of contraceptives. Much of the available data stems from studies that don't always account for generational differences or long-term tracking. This gap in research leaves a legacy of uncertainty, urging a need for comprehensive studies that span lifetimes rather than limited timeframes.

In understanding the diverse implications of the pill, one must also examine the intersection of culture and medicine. Society's acceptance and advocacy for the pill are deeply intertwined with the evolving roles of women. While the aim is empowerment, it risks overlooking the nuanced and often individualized impact on health and well-being. The pill's long-term effects serve as an invitation to critically evaluate how medical advances balance with human health and dignity.

What emerges from examining these long-term health implications is more than an inventory of side effects; it is a call to action. Women and society must engage more deeply with the conversation around reproductive health choices, seeking pathways that prioritize both the physical and emotional integrity of individuals. Health care providers, too, play a crucial role in providing informed, empathetic guidance that respects each woman's unique narrative.

- Increased awareness of potential risks and side effects among women and practitioners.
- Prioritizing research that addresses gaps in understanding long-term health outcomes.
- Advocacy for personalized health care approaches that respect diverse experiences.
- Encouraging environmental responsibility in pharmaceutical practices.

If the pill represents a cornerstone of modern reproductive liberty, then its hidden dangers summon us towards a holistic understanding of freedom —one that includes awareness and informed choice. The balance between utility and danger isn't static; it beckons us towards an ethical dialogue where health is central and deeply human. In the grand tapestry of medical innovation, these long-term implications offer threads of caution and promise, woven into the larger narrative of what it means to advance while safeguarding the very essence of life itself.

Chapter 5: Societal Impact of Abortion

The societal impact of abortion isn't just a collection of statistics but a woven tapestry of human experiences affecting the family unit and community frameworks. Every terminated pregnancy echoes in population dynamics, subtly influencing demographic shifts and societal constructs in ways both profound and unsettling. Economically, the decision holds ramifications, as potential contributors to future economies are lost, altering labor markets and generational wealth transfers. The moral fabric of society is also tested, as ethical discussions ignite passionate debates on life, choice, and responsibility, each leaving an indelible mark on cultural conscience. Moreover, it strains social systems designed to support life, fostering a dystopian reality where the value of life is often diminished to an abstract statistic rather than a tangible potential. This chapter seeks to unravel these influences, inviting a deeper reflection on how abortion enmeshes with societal evolution and the values we hold dear.

Abortion's Influence on Population Dynamics

The topic of abortion is fraught with complexities, weaving into the very fabric of population dynamics and societal progression. As the practice of abortion proliferates across cultures and nations, its repercussions on population growth cannot be dismissed lightly. From an ethical standpoint, the implications of widespread abortion practices influence not only the immediate community but also the future of the global population. The moral fabric of society is subtly yet dramatically altered whenever potential life is prematurely ended.

One must consider how population statistics have been, and continue to be, shaped by the prevalence of abortion. Where there are fewer births, the age demographics of a nation can skew towards an aging populace, resulting in significant challenges for economies built on the presumption of continual growth and development. This situation presents a dystopian plight for future generations, who may be burdened by the responsibilities of an increasingly top-heavy population pyramid. The individual's potential—what they might have contributed to the world—is lost each time a decision is made to terminate a gestation.

The role of abortion in population dynamics is, in part, an extension of choices manifested through personal, societal, and governmental policies. In many countries, policy-makers have attempted to adapt to these changing demographics through incentives to encourage births. History bears witness to this strategy, where nations grappling with population decline resort to monetary benefits and other incentives to induce higher birth rates. Yet, these efforts often prove insufficient when ideological shifts about the sanctity of life maintain a stronghold on societal attitudes.

Furthermore, the impact of abortion on population dynamics can also be seen through the lens of familial structures and social relationships. Families, which historically have been seen as the cornerstone of societal development, find their dynamics altered when abortion becomes a common recourse. A family's potential for expansion is curtailed, altering community traditions and leaving an indelible mark on cultural continuity.

There are also broader considerations, such as the economic ramifications of reduced population growth due to abortion. A diminished birth rate can lead to a constricted labor force, exerting pressure on the social systems that support the elderly and the vulnerable. Economic stability, often taken as a given in prosperous nations, becomes precarious when job markets cannot be sustained by a youth dearth. Families once buoyed by the prospect of robust future generations may face the harrowing impact of decisions made in the present.

Conversely, as some advocates argue, abortion can sometimes act as a regulator within population dynamics, theoretically alleviating the resource strains of a burgeoning populace. However, this line of reasoning poses profound ethical questions: does the alleviation of certain societal pressures justify the act of ending a nascent life? This quandary pokes at the very heart of moral philosophy and forces society to confront its values and priorities head-on.

From a Roman Catholic perspective, the inviolability of life is paramount. Historical texts and teachings from the Church emphasize respect for life from conception to natural death. This belief is not only spiritual but deeply interwoven with arguments about human dignity and the role of divine providence in the unfolding tapestry of human existence. The challenge, then, is maintaining this respect amid a landscape where secular ideologies often clash with religious and ethical values.

There are wider responses on this issue as well. Across various nations, cultural attitudes towards abortion and population control are influenced by governmental and religious directives as much as by indigenous customs and economic status. In some societies, abortion is heavily restricted, and the drive to maintain population growth is fierce, often encouraged by both spiritual doctrine and national policy.

With each choice to abort comes a ripple effect, touching those indirectly involved in deeply personal ways. The societal collective conscience absorbs these choices, influencing the moral and spiritual health of communities and nations. One could say that the presence of abortion shifts how life itself is valued, creating lasting impressions on population dynamics and human relations.

Ultimately, the intersection of abortion and population dynamics is interlaced with questions of ethics, governance, and theology. As humanity strides bravely into an unpredictable future, haunted by the spectres of past decisions, the question remains: how will society reckon with the overlooked lives, the silent testimonies of potential undone, and the enduring chasm between sacred life and societal desires? By examining these intersections, we hold a mirror to our collective conscience and face the challenge of reconciling our responsibilities to each nascent soul and the future world they might have helped shape.

Economic Consequences

Abortion, beyond its profound moral and ethical discourse, presents a consequential economic dimension that reverberates across society like an echo in a vast canyon. The decision to terminate a potential life invokes a cascade of economic reactions, affecting not just the individuals directly involved but also the broader societal framework. From the reverberations in labor markets to the implications for social welfare systems, the economic consequences of abortion are as far-reaching as they are complex.

The contemporary economy thrives on the dynamics of population growth and demographic shifts. A society's economic vitality is intimately tied to its population structure; hence, abortion's influence on population dynamics bears significant economic ramifications. When unborn children are denied the breath of life, they also forgo becoming integral cogs in the machinery of economic productivity and consumption. This has potential long-term implications for the workforce, leading to an aging population without the balance of youthful vigor to sustain economic progress.

Yet, the economic consequences can't merely be reduced to calculations of population numbers. The ripple effect touches labor force participation, particularly of women, and consequently, household incomes. Women who choose abortion often cite economic hardship and the inability to provide for a child as primary reasons for their decision. This, however, places them in a paradoxical situation, as the cycle of economic struggle is perpetuated within systems that offer insufficient support for working mothers. If such systemic support were enhanced, perhaps the economic calculations leading to the choice of abortion would be significantly altered.

Further complicating this economic landscape is the cost burden carried by healthcare systems. The immediate medical costs of abortion procedures may seem straightforward, yet they belie the potential for long-term healthcare demands stemming from physical or psychological complications. Societal expenditures in this regard can snowball over time, manifesting in increased demands on public mental health services and other community supports. Moreover, the absence of a child marginally reduces future investment in areas such as education and child care, ultimately stagnating sectors of the economy reliant on youthful participation and growth.

Consider the economic implications for social security and retirement systems. These systems, fundamental pillars of social welfare, thrive on the influx of a young, working-age population to support the increasingly aging populace. The deferment of births through abortion decisions strips these systems of potential contributors, creating a demographic imbalance that challenges their sustainability over time. The irony lies in the fact that many abortion decisions are predicated on immediate economic distress, yet they contribute to long-term economic instability.

The economic consequences ripple into corporate and industrial dimensions as well. Industries that rely on the perpetual cycle of birth—such as those producing child-focused goods and services—are indirectly affected. A reduction in birth rates can lead to a contraction in these markets, affecting jobs and economic output. The creation and consumption of goods designed for children and families generate substantial economic activity, and a diminishment in this cycle causes reverberations that can dampen economic vigor.

Moreover, it's crucial to acknowledge the fiscal influence of the abortion industry itself. With its significant financial footprint, the industry shifts economic resources that might otherwise nourish different forms of healthcare or social support systems. Resources channeled into the facilitation and advocacy of abortion services bear their own set of economic calculations, impacting taxpayer allocations, and influencing healthcare policy debates.

On an individual level, economists might attempt to quantify the lost potential earnings across a lifetime for each aborted child, an exercise fraught with moral considerations yet one that starkly highlights the financial potential unrealized. This unrealized potential can equate to untapped innovations, unfulfillable job roles, and an absence of societal contributions that might have otherwise emerged from each lost life.

Thus, while some argue that abortion alleviates immediate economic burdens on individuals overwhelmed by the financial implications of parenthood, it is also true that these decisions resonate beyond the immediate, reshaping economic landscapes in ways both seen and unseen. Abortion may address an immediate economic hardship for the individual, but the collective economy bears its shadow for years, if not decades, to come, challenging societal structures that many rely on for security and prosperity.

As we ponder the economic consequences of abortion within a world increasingly interconnected by commerce and capital, let us not be blind to the multifaceted realities that underscore these economic trends. Abortion does not exist in an economic vacuum; it permeates various strata of society and leaves in its wake questions that economies, policymakers, and individuals must continually wrestle with. It is imperative to consider not only the moral and personal dimensions but also the substantial economic consequences that shape the future fabric of our global society.

Chapter 6: Abortion and Women's Health

The debate surrounding abortion isn't just a matter of moral and ethical contemplation—it has profound implications on women's health, both physically and mentally. In a society grappling with the dichotomy of choice and consequence, women's well-being often finds itself caught in the crossfire. Abortion can have significant physical repercussions, affecting a woman's body in ways that are not always immediately apparent but can manifest over time, altering the life and health trajectory of many. Mental health challenges often shadow the physical ones, with emotions ranging from relief to profound regret, impacting familial ties and individual peace. This chapter delves into these complex and often overlooked dimensions, challenging the narrative fostered by proponents of abortion who highlight autonomy without accounting for its full spectrum of consequences. By revealing the truths about abortion's impact on women's health, we aim to foster a deeper understanding of the stakes involved, encouraging a societal shift towards genuine care and informed compassion.

Physical Implications of Abortion

Abortion, a procedure that has been performed for centuries, varies starkly in its physical implications, often dependent on medical practices, gestational stage, and individual health conditions. Physical consequences differ significantly between surgical and medical abortions, each carrying inherent risks. Yet, the idyllic promises of safety and simplicity underscored by the industry sometimes fail to align with the reality many women face.

The physical aftermath for women often begins with the procedure itself. Surgical abortions, commonly performed in the first trimester, include methods like suction aspiration or dilation and curettage. These procedures can lead to immediate complications such as excessive bleeding, infection, or damage to the uterus or other organs. Even in the best facilities, with the most skilled practitioners, there's no absolute guarantee against these adverse outcomes. Indeed, the cloak of clinical cleanliness may mask the inherent violence each procedure enacts on a woman's body.

Meanwhile, medical abortions, heralded as a less invasive option, primarily involve pharmaceuticals like mifepristone and misoprostol. Despite their non-surgical nature, these drugs can initiate severe cramping, nausea, and heavy bleeding. Recent studies suggest these effects are not trivial. They contribute to the growing number of emergency room visits post-abortion, a statistic often overlooked in the broader discourse. What begins as a seemingly straightforward ingestion of a pill can spiral into a nightmarish ordeal, alienating a woman from her own body while promising her control.

Beyond the immediate risks, there's a spectrum of long-term physical consequences that warrant attention. The reproductive system, once interfered with so drastically, may not emerge unscathed. Potential complications for future pregnancies include preterm birth, low birth weight, and placental abnormalities. Such implications may not be widely known or acknowledged, yet they shadow every subsequent gynecological and obstetric appointment, an unwelcome reminder of a decision that was supposed to liberate rather than imprison.

Moreover, conditions like Asherman's syndrome—a formation of scar tissue in the uterus—have been directly linked to surgical abortions. They manifest as chronic pelvic pain, irregular menstruation, and, in severe cases, infertility. For many women, this isn't merely a physical ailment; it's a lingering question to which the industry offers no satisfying answer.

Of course, the breast cancer debate adds another layer of complexity. While it remains contentious, proponents of the link between abortion and increased breast cancer risk point to the biological changes the breast undergoes during pregnancy. Interrupting this natural progression prematurely can, theoretically, increase susceptibility to carcinogens. Although comprehensive studies investigating this potential risk are still evolving, the mere association introduces another unsettling dimension to the consequences of abortion.

In addition, the overall impact on women's health doesn't exist in a vacuum. The ripple effects extend beyond individual bodies, contributing fundamentally to family dynamics, societal health, and generational wellness. It's an intersection where physical health and societal values collide, presenting an area rich for further exploration yet too often sidelined in mainstream debates.

From a perspective deeply seated in Roman Catholic teachings, the sanctity of life and the integrity of the human body intertwine. The physical implications of abortion cannot be isolated from the soul's travails, and vice versa. Even Saint Thomas Aquinas' philosophies underscore the interconnectedness of body and soul, hinting at a deeper depreciation when the physical form is subjected to such irreversible interventions.

Understanding these consequences within a historical context offers a grim reminder of recurring patterns and unlearned lessons. Societies that have normalized abortion often experience deeper physical and moral crises, evidence of a relentless cycle perpetuated by scientific advancements misaligned with ethical compass. It's a cautionary narrative, one that implores reflection amidst the medicalization of human elements once considered sacred.

Let's not ignore the voices of women who, having experienced these physical repercussions firsthand, become advocates for change. Their bodies bear the silent testimony of procedures once deemed harmless, yet which left indelible marks beyond scars. Through their stories, they articulate an often-overlooked truth: the human body is not a wasteland for seemingly benign medical interventions; it is a reflection of divine artistry that demands respect and reverence.

In sum, the physical implications of abortion go far beyond statistics and clinical observations. They encapsulate a broader narrative of human struggle, bodily integrity, and societal values. As we strive to comprehend these complexities, let's remember the profound duty of safeguarding human life at all stages, honoring the harmonious design we each embody.

Mental Health Challenges

The intricate tapestry of a woman's mental health is woven delicately, often teetering on the edge of vulnerability when faced with profound life decisions such as abortion. This chapter delves into the silent, rarely acknowledged strife endured by many women who have walked this path. The emotional turmoil accompanying such profound choices can have long-lasting effects, stretching beyond the immediate aftermath and into the very essence of one's being.

Research and anecdotal evidence alike have highlighted an array of mental health challenges that surface post-abortion. Women may experience a range of emotions, from relief and sadness to guilt and depression. For some, these feelings coalesce into a lasting psychological shadow, casting a pall over their mental health. Unavoidable questions linger: "What if?" and "Should I have made a different choice?" These questions often spiral into cycles of anxiety and regret that are difficult to escape.

Beyond the immediate emotional aftermath, some women encounter more severe conditions, such as Post-Traumatic Stress Disorder (PTSD), anxiety disorders, and depression. The mental health community continues to explore these connections, and while the findings are varied, it is evident that many women grapple with these issues silently, receiving little understanding from a society that often downplays their struggles.

Adding to the weight of their burden, many women feel isolated in their pain. Cultural and familial expectations can make discussing their psychological state difficult. In some cases, there is an overwhelming stigma attached to seeking help, driven by fear of judgment or ostracism. Catholic women might feel a heightened tension between their religious convictions and the decision they've made, further complicating their healing process.

The Catholic Church, with its deep-rooted beliefs about the sanctity of life, plays a crucial role in shaping the narratives and perceptions around abortion. For devout believers, the decision to terminate a pregnancy is not just personal but a significant moral conflict, one that could weigh heavily on their conscience. Saint Thomas Aquinas spoke of the soul's light, but many women find their spiritual luminosity dimmed by guilt and sorrow.

In striving for a harmonious reconciliation between faith and experience, Roman Catholic women are faced with a dual struggle. The need for spiritual healing becomes urgent, as does the necessity for acknowledgment and pastoral care within their communities. The Church's role in offering compassionate support cannot be underestimated, as it is in these moments of crisis that the teachings of love, understanding, and redemption must shine brightest. Pope Saint John Paul II often emphasized the importance of forgiveness and mercy—a beacon for those seeking solace.

Moreover, women who undergo abortions often face a societal dichotomy —being told on one hand that it should be empowering or liberating, while simultaneously feeling judged or pitied by others. This contradiction only adds layers to the mental health challenges they confront. The conflict between societal attitudes and personal grief can lead to feelings of disenfranchisement, a sense of not being understood or supported.

GK Chesterton once opined on the paradoxes of modern life, and within these mental health challenges lies just such a paradox. Women are caught in a paradoxical storm of expected emancipation and personal adversity, trying to navigate an environment that celebrates freedom of choice yet often disregards the emotional aftermath of those choices.

It's important for families, friends, and communities to recognize the potential mental health repercussions of abortion and foster environments of support rather than judgment. This support is vital in helping women address and heal from any psychological distress. Support groups, counseling, and spiritual guidance should be accessible and devoid of stigma, allowing women the space to breathe, reflect, and heal.

While the discourse on abortion frequently focuses on physical health and legal rights, mental health considerations must not be marginalized. Too often, the narrative around abortion is polarized, leaving little space for nuanced discussions about its emotional ramifications. By bringing these mental health challenges to light, we can move towards a society that acknowledges the full spectrum of abortion's impact on women's health and endeavors to help those in need of care and understanding.

To build a future that honors both choice and well-being, it is essential to advocate for comprehensive mental health support systems. Initiatives that prioritize emotional recovery and offer solace to those affected by abortion can pave the way for healing and reconciliation. In this, we find not a dystopian world of abandonment but a utopian vision of caring and community. Let us embark on this journey of understanding, courage, and compassion, and ensure that no woman feels alone in her post-abortion experience.

Chapter 7: The Emotional Toll on Families

In the quiet aftermath of an abortion, the emotional ripples extend far beyond the individual, often touching the fragile threads that bind families together. This chapter delves into the complex emotional landscape that emerges, weaving a narrative of unseen scars and strained relationships. Families, drawn into the orbit of this choice, may face a mosaic of emotions ranging from unspoken grief to lingering guilt, challenging the very foundation of their bonds. The silent echoes of what might have been create a shadow that colors interactions, perhaps sowing seeds of discord or isolation. Yet, within the struggle, there lies an opportunity for healing and understanding—a call to acknowledge and address the emotional realities that many endure in solitude. Coping mechanisms vary, with some families turning inward, navigating this shared burden with quiet resilience, while others may fracture, unable to reconcile their pain. By unmasking these hidden tolls, we can foster a path to empathy and support, recognizing that true healing involves the entire familial tapestry.

Effects on Relationships

Abortion, as a deeply personal experience, undeniably leaves its imprint on the fabric of relationships. In the intimate realm of family, its effects can ripple through the hearts and lives of all members. These ripples can often turn into waves, reshaping the bonds that unite a family. The process, decision, and aftermath of abortion introduce elements of tension, guilt, sorrow, and sometimes relief, each weaving itself into the tapestry of familial connections.

Consider, for a moment, the relationship between partners. For many, the discovery of an unplanned pregnancy is a pivotal moment that tests trust and commitment. In such circumstances, abortion can become not only a personal choice but a shared decision fraught with mutual anxieties and expectations. Partners might find their connection strained as they navigate complex emotional landscapes. Some may experience a profound sense of loss that lingers beneath the surface, manifesting in ways they may not fully understand. This unseen burden may cause distances to widen over time, as intimacy gives way to silence.

Yet, it is not only between couples that we observe these effects. The extended family—siblings, parents, even close friends—feels this impact too. Take, for instance, the sense of shared mourning that can affect a family when a sibling chooses abortion. Brothers and sisters might feel an unnameable sadness for the loss of a potential niece or nephew, their understanding often muffled by societal norms that discourage open dialogue on such matters. Parents might wrestle with conflict, caught between their empathy for their child's difficult choice and personal beliefs that may be at odds with that decision.

For parents, the challenge is intricate. Their roles as caregivers often conflict with the vast gulf between generational views on abortion. What some might see as an act of autonomy and freedom, others view as a moral transgression. This dichotomy can create emotional schisms within the family unit, leading to conversations laden with tension or avoidance. More often than not, discussions are hushed tones at the dining table, or unspoken thoughts echoing in the corridors, creating an environment that can feel both isolating and unwelcoming.

However, with open communication and understanding, these challenging moments can also evolve into opportunities for reconciliation and growth. Families who confront these issues head-on, embracing the complexities of their emotions, may find pathways to rebuild their relationships. It's in the quiet acceptance of human frailty and the active pursuit of forgiveness that they can begin to heal the wounds left by such critical choices.

The Church, too, plays a pivotal role in this emotional milieu. Roman Catholic teachings, with their emphasis on the sanctity of life, often influence how families process the experience of abortion. For believers, this can create a dilemma, torn between adherence to doctrine and the unconditional love they strive to practice. The teachings of the Church provide a framework for compassion and forgiveness, urging families to seek solace in shared faith and collective healing.

Yet, the burden of abortion on relationships extends beyond immediate families. Communities, too, bear witness to the subtle rifts that such personal decisions can engender. Friends who once shared collective hopes and dreams may find themselves on opposing sides of ethical and moral debates. The friction of differing worldviews can strain old friendships, leaving individuals feeling marooned in their own convictions.

Through all this, there exists a hope that resonates within the hearts of those seeking redemption and understanding. The interplay between decision and emotion, loss and recovery, does not have to undermine the bonds that unite us. Instead, it can compel families and communities to lean into resilience, embracing the Catholic tradition of forgiveness and grace.

In the end, while abortion has the potential to delineate stark boundaries within relationships, it also offers a chance for profound introspection and healing. As families grapple with the heavy cost of these decisions, they engage in the deeper work of understanding each other's silences, gestures, and the words that linger unspoken. It's in this space that new narratives emerge—ones that are nourished by patience and compassion, and that recognize the inherent dignity of every human emotion.

Therefore, the role of faith, introspection, and the willingness to engage in transformative dialogue becomes crucial. Here, one finds the possibility of not just mending broken ties but cultivating a stronger, more empathetic bond. The true essence of a family forged through such trials is one where love prevails—a love that, much like gold refined by fire, is made purer by its experiences.

Coping With Post-Abortion Trauma

The decision to undergo an abortion can ripple through the fabric of a family's emotional landscape, leaving threads of trauma, guilt, and grief that are often hard to untangle. The impact of this choice is profound, and the emotional upheaval that follows can feel like a storm, shaking the foundations of relationships and personal identity. Coping with post-abortion trauma is a journey fraught with complexity and requires understanding, forgiveness, and support. Every story is unique, yet certain themes resonate across many experiences.

One key aspect of post-abortion trauma is the silence that often surrounds it. Families may struggle with an inability to communicate effectively about their emotions, creating an environment where feelings of isolation flourish. This silence stems, in part, from societal stigma and the fear of judgment. The decision is deeply personal, yet it carries a public shadow. It can be difficult for individuals to find allies in their healing journey when they wrestle with internalized shame.

Breaking this silence is an essential step in healing. Open and compassionate dialogue can act as a balm, allowing those affected to voice their pain and begin processing their emotions. Couples need to foster an environment where each person feels safe to express guilt, sorrow, or even relief without fear of reproach. Religious and community leaders often play a critical role in facilitating these conversations, offering perspectives that blend faith and empathy.

From a Catholic viewpoint, the sanctity of life is a guiding principle, and while this belief may intensify feelings of remorse post-abortion, it also offers pathways to healing and redemption. The concepts of confession, penance, and divine forgiveness are not merely ritualistic but are powerful tools in the personal reclamation of peace. In moments of despair, reaching towards these spiritual aids can provide a necessary anchor in turbulent emotional seas.

Alongside spiritual guidance, professional counseling can be instrumental in addressing post-abortion trauma. Mental health professionals trained in post-abortion counseling provide a space where feelings can be untangled and processed. This therapeutic relationship facilitates progress from emotional paralysis to a more resilient state of being. Counseling helps individuals develop coping strategies tailored to their unique emotional needs, providing them with the tools to navigate their new reality.

For many, the path to recovery involves reconnecting with their faith or rediscovering spiritual practices that had once been comforting. Engaging in community rituals, prayer, or spiritual retreats can offer solace and a sense of belonging. These activities emphasize that healing is not a solitary journey but one that thrives with communal support and understanding.

While personal and familial healing are crucial, society at large must also engage with these themes of trauma and recovery. Dystopian realities arise when communities fail to address the emotional aftermath of abortion, perpetuating cycles of grief and isolation. It is imperative for societal structures to be set in place that provide expansive support networks, facilitating not just individual healing but communal resilience as well.

Appreciating the profound impact of abortion on families can illuminate a path forward in a more empathetic and supportive societal landscape. By weaving together personal stories and community responses, a utopian vision emerges where post-abortion care is holistic and comprehensive. In this world, every individual finds a network ready to hold, uplift, and guide them towards healing—a world where prohibition transforms not through dictation but through a collective embrace of life's sanctity and a unified resolve not to leave anyone behind in despair.

Chapter 8: The Abortion Industry's Hidden Agendas

Building upon the intricate narratives of previous discussions, the abortion industry's hidden agendas reveal unsettling truths that demand our scrutiny. Behind the veneer of healthcare lies a complex web interwoven with eugenic ideologies and targeted campaigns that surreptitiously influence societal structures. These agendas often masquerade as empowerment, yet they camouflage intentions that subtly shape demographics, especially among the youth and marginalized communities. It's not merely a matter of choice but rather an intricate dance of power and control, steering societal norms toward a future that consciously or unconsciously marginalizes the vulnerable. The shadows of history echo these patterns, where past eugenic philosophies resurface in modern guises, leaving us to ponder the ethical implications of such concealed motives. By unraveling these agendas, we begin to understand the broader implications for families, communities, and individual dignity, urging a collective reflection on the moral compass that guides societal choices.

Exploring Eugenic Roots

The abortion industry, often cloaked in the language of choice and personal freedom, harbors origins that are both unsettling and deeply entwined with the eugenics movement. To understand how these eugenic ideas came to influence abortion practices, we need to delve into the 19th and early 20th centuries, a period teeming with scientific curiosity but also with disturbing reflections on human worth and societal progress. During this time, the concept of "better breeding" gained traction, purporting a future where genetic selection could refine the human race, discarding those deemed unfit. **Though the scientific veneer seemed progressive, the underlying motives were anything but benign.**

Eugenics, a term coined by Sir Francis Galton, emerged as a pseudo-scientific movement aimed at improving the hereditary quality of humans. The belief was that society could accelerate natural selection through controlled human reproduction. As unsettling as these ideas were, they found fertile ground not only in academic circles but in public policy. Prominent figures, including some well-respected scientists and policy makers, zealously advocated for measures that would curb the reproduction of individuals deemed "inferior." In the grim shadow of such rationale, abortion was seen as a tool to achieve these ends—a means to manage and engineer the population.

The echo of these eugenic ideas can still be heard today, reverberating through policies and rhetoric that subtly, and sometimes overtly, suggest that certain lives are less worthy. One need not look too far into the past to observe when this ideology reached its apex in such tragic, historic episodes like the sterilization movements where thousands, often poor and minority women, were stripped of their reproductive rights. This was orchestrated under the guise of public good, cloaked in the chilling language of "racial hygiene."

Margaret Sanger, a prominent figure in the birth control movement and the founder of what would become Planned Parenthood, held views that were closely aligned with eugenic thought. *She believed that reproductive control was essential in crafting a more 'fit' nation.* While her contributions to birth control are often highlighted, **it's essential to remember her support for eugenics policies that sought to curb the birthrate of those she deemed unfit.** Today, many disassociate these unsettling origins from modern practices, yet the legacy often influences subtle biases within reproductive health narratives.

This intersection of eugenics and abortion raises harrowing questions about equality and moral ethics that we must confront. Historians and those examining the abortion industry's hidden agendas cannot overlook the deliberate targeting of specific populations—primarily those marginalized—by abortion proponents. It's a haunting portrayal of how dehumanizing beliefs can shape policies that impact millions under the veneer of choice and autonomy.

The consequences of this eugenic ideology on abortion extend beyond individual rights to the larger societal framework. Once we entertain the notion that some lives are less worthy, it opens the door to a dystopian society that implicitly values efficiency and productivity over the inherent dignity shared by every human being. Aborting a fetus based on genetic traits or potential disabilities is a slippery slope that echoes the dark chapters of history, where unsolicited decisions were made over who deserves to procreate and who does not.

Yet, this isn't merely a matter of looking back. It's about identifying the remnants of this ideology in modern practices and discourses. As we examine the routes that policies and societal attitudes take, historical awareness is a necessary lens through which we can recognize and correct these biases. An authentic commitment to life affirms that every individual, regardless of their genetic makeup or social standing, possesses an irreplaceable value that no one should have the power to diminish.

As Catholics, historians, and engaged citizens, it's our duty to scrutinize how these past and present ties between abortion and eugenics threaten our moral fabric and communal values. Abortion isn't just about choice; it's deeply entangled with narratives that once sought to re-engineer society through exclusion. By understanding these connections, we can advocate for policies and practices rooted in true respect for human life, lighting the path toward a utopian vision where every life is cherished as a miraculous part of the tapestry of humanity.

Targeting Youth and Minorities

The abortion industry's calculated targeting of youth and minorities raises significant ethical and moral questions, as it strips away the innocence and potential of vulnerable groups. There exists a pervasive narrative, subtly monitored and directed, that seeks to normalize the practice of abortion within these demographics. This narrative often employs a mix of supposed empowerment and healthcare rhetoric to mask a darker, underlying agenda.

A troubling aspect of this focus is how it intertwines with systemic societal inequalities. By aiming abortion services at minorities, particularly African American and Hispanic communities, there's an implicit message that these lives are less valuable or undesired. Historical roots in eugenics further taint these practices, making the moral landscape vertiginous. It's not just a social issue; it's a deeply spiritual one, calling into question the intrinsic value assigned to human life.

One might ponder why these communities? The answer lies in the intersection of race, socio-economic challenges, and a lack of access to alternative healthcare and support systems. Predominantly minority neighborhoods often boast a disproportionately high number of family planning clinics offering abortion services. The consequence is clear: a conveniently accessible option with far-reaching implications for the fabric of these communities.

Moreover, in targeting young people, the industry preys on a demographic often still forming their identities and worldviews. Through aggressive marketing strategies, cloaked educational programs, and even peer-influenced discussions, abortion is sold as empowerment, a rite of passage into modern maturity. Yet this is far from the truth. The decision carries profound personal and societal consequences, frequently leaving emotional scars and moral quandaries that clash with developmental growth.

Furthermore, educational programs are controversial as they frequently promote a range of reproductive health options without fully elucidating the potential risks or ethical concerns associated with abortion. They cleverly blend in health education curriculums, presenting abortion as just another healthcare decision, devoid of its moral gravity. This creates an illusion of choice that lacks informed consent, as young people are not typically equipped to process the potential ramifications on their futures or their souls.

Perhaps the most disheartening aspect is the stripping away of community support and familial discussions. When abortion becomes the easily accessible, socially approved solution, it undermines traditional family and community roles in guiding young people through difficult choices. The result is an erosion of community bonds and a drift towards individualism that celebrates choice over responsibility, momentary relief over long-term considerations.

In minorities, the impact is compounded by systemic obstacles that appear insurmountable. These communities, often fighting battles on multiple fronts, find themselves caught in a cycle reinforced by the abortion industry's deliberate positioning within their borders. Such targeting exacerbates poverty and limits opportunities for breaking free from the cycle of socio-economic underachievement.

The industry's approach also perpetuates divisive stereotypes. It's part of a broader socio-political strategy that perpetuates racial and economic discrimination, inevitably impacting society's view of ethnic minorities. While the guise is healthcare access and choice, the deeper agenda is arguably about control and managing population dynamics. This control masquerades as progressive policy but is inherently regressive, stifling growth and perpetuating inequality.

What might a future look like where this targeting ceases? Imagine a world where every community, including youth and minorities, has access to comprehensive support systems that prioritize life and well-being. Here, informed choices, rooted in a rich understanding of human dignity and respect for life, define the process of decision-making. Such a future requires significant changes in societal structures, economies, and values.

It's crucial to advocate for educational and health systems that acknowledge and address their roles in this narrative. Schools and communities should focus on equipping youth with the tools to face life's challenges without resorting to solutions that undermine their potential. This involves promoting a culture of life, where every decision considers its effects on personal development and societal well-being.

As we grapple with these realities, the importance of moral guidance and societal accountability becomes clear. Catholic teachings emphasize the sanctity of life, encouraging communities to promote life-affirming alternatives. This invites a broader conversation about how we, as a society, value and protect the innocence and potential of our young and minority populations. In doing so, we challenge the industry's hidden agendas and work towards a society that celebrates life in all its forms.

Chapter 9: Abortion's Ethical and Moral Dimensions

The ethical and moral dimensions of abortion often bring into sharp relief the intricate tapestry of values and beliefs that define human experience. For Roman Catholics, acquainted with the doctrine of the sanctity of life, the topic isn't merely an abstract debate but a journey into the very essence of existence and divine obedience. Here lies a fundamental quandary that has persisted through time: how do we reconcile individual autonomy with the collective moral compass that seeks to protect life at its most vulnerable stage? The quandary extends to medical practitioners who grapple with their dual roles as healers and providers of choice, nudging them into ethical crosswinds. As society treads this delicate terrain, it's essential to reflect not just on religious teachings but also on the holistic ramifications—how such choices reverberate through families and communities, sometimes sowing seeds of division and sorrow. Contemporary moral philosophy urges a re-engagement with these profound questions, prompting historians to trace the evolution of thought and, more basically, how society's ethos shapes and is shaped by the choices it ultimately endorses or condemns. This complex interplay of beliefs, practice, and consequence serves as a reminder of our shared responsibility to seek a compassionate resolution that honors both life and personal conscience within the societal mosaic.

Religious Perspectives on Abortion

In the labyrinth of ethical debates and moral quandaries, the question of abortion looms with a particular weight. From a religious perspective, one's stance on abortion is often rooted in deep-seated beliefs about the sanctity of life. This viewpoint isn't merely a matter of doctrine but a reflection of the broader vision of life and human dignity. For Roman Catholics, as well as adherents of many other faith traditions, the discussion encompasses more than the act itself; it delves into the very essence of human existence and the divine imprint upon it.

The Roman Catholic Church, with its extensive theological tradition, stands firm against abortion. Grounded in the belief that life begins at conception, this opposition is more than doctrinal—it is a profound declaration of the inherent value of every human being. This perspective is not simply a set of rules imposed from above but is intricately woven into the fabric of Catholic social teaching, which places a paramount emphasis on the dignity of the human person. For Catholics, then, abortion is not seen as just a medical or personal choice but a moral violation, a transgression against the inviolable sanctity of human life.

In tracing the Catholic viewpoint, one must consider the words of Pope Saint John Paul II, who poignantly described the modern "culture of death" in his encyclical *Evangelium Vitae* (The Gospel of Life). He argued that society's acceptance of abortion reflects a grave loss of respect for human dignity. With his characteristic passion and clarity, he called for a culture of life, one that upholds every human life with care and reverence. Such a stance draws heavily on the rich philosophical heritage of figures like Saint Thomas Aquinas, who articulated the principles of natural law. Aquinas asserted that the good of the human person is achieved by living in accordance with reason enlightened by faith, and by this view, protecting life from its inception is not merely a religious duty but a moral imperative dictated by natural reason.

Beyond Catholicism, other religious traditions also weigh in on the moral dimensions of abortion, albeit sometimes with variegated nuances. Within

Christianity, Protestants exhibit a range of interpretations. While some denominations, like Evangelicals, echo the Catholic emphasis on life beginning at conception, others may allow for more nuanced positions, particularly in complex medical or moral situations. In these contexts, the decision may hinge on pastoral guidance and the individual's conscience.

Judaism generally permits abortion, especially if the mother's life is at risk, emphasizing the health and wellbeing of the mother. The Talmud and subsequent rabbinic interpretations have historically grappled with these issues in depth, often underlining the potential life rather than the actualized one. This perspective doesn't disregard the potentiality of the unborn, but it holds a nuanced approach considering the circumstances surrounding each case. Such a view emerges from a long tradition of interpretation and debate over scriptural texts, exemplifying Judaism's intricate balance between law, ethics, and compassion.

Islamic teachings, too, provide a perspective on abortion that is both principled and nuanced. While generally opposing abortion, Islamic jurisprudence allows for exceptions, particularly if the mother's life is endangered or in cases of severe fetal abnormalities. The principles guiding these decisions are based on the *Sharia*, which underscores the protection and preservation of life but also the necessity to act with compassion and mercy. The emphasis lies in weighing the circumstances and seeking the guidance of moral principles deeply rooted in the faith's theological framework.

For Hinduism, the sanctity of life is paramount, often linking abortion to the spiritual ramifications of one's actions, or karma. Life is considered sacred, and thus, the act of terminating a fetus is generally viewed in a negative light. However, the diverse interpretations among Hindu scholars and the contextual considerations often lead to a variety of perspectives within the broader Hindu community.

Buddhism presents another distinctive view, stressing the cycle of life, death, and rebirth. Abortion is typically discouraged because it interrupts the cycle of *samsara*, but like other faiths, there may be allowances made in dire circumstances. Central to Buddhist ethics is the importance of intention and compassion, reflecting a complex interplay between moral rules and the guiding principle of reducing suffering.

Despite these varied religious perspectives, what binds them is a profound respect for life and the moral dimensions it encompasses. The dialogue between different religious traditions and their teachings on abortion shows that this issue transcends mere policy debates and enters the realm of profound existential and ethical reflection. It reveals humanity's ongoing quest to understand and defend the dignity of life amidst diverse cultural and spiritual landscapes.

While each religious tradition offers its unique guidance on the topic, they all grapple with the same existential questions: What constitutes the beginning of life? What are the moral responsibilities of individuals? How do we balance compassion with adherence to ethical principles? As they wrestle with these questions, their teachings serve as a beacon for many who seek to navigate the complexities of life and death with a conscience formed by faith and reason.

In these debates, it becomes evident that religion does not merely dictate rules; it inspires. It calls communities to a higher vision where the protection of life is seen not as a limitation but as a liberating affirmation of our shared humanity. Here, the religious perspectives on abortion converge as they remind society of the broader implications of justice, mercy, and the altogether incontrovertible sanctity of life.

Moral Dilemmas Faced by Medical Practitioners

Within the sterile walls of medical institutions, where the promise of healing stands tall, practitioners often face moral dilemmas that test their convictions and values. Abortion, more than any other procedure, raises profound ethical questions that don't merely demand medical expertise but scrape the very core of morality and conscience. Medical practitioners, particularly those holding strong religious beliefs such as Roman Catholics, find themselves at a crossroads where their professional obligations might starkly contrast with their personal moral and ethical beliefs. These dilemmas often permeate their thoughts, casting long shadows over their practice.

On one hand, doctors are bound by the Hippocratic Oath, a pledge to do no harm and always act in the patient's best interest. For many, this commitment conflicts with participating in or facilitating abortions. They may perceive the procedure as contradictory to the essence of their role as healers, particularly when considering the unborn child as a life deserving protection. The act of ending a potential life, rather than preserving it, can haunt the conscience of those who are steadfast in seeing humanity in the unborn.

Moreover, the pressure from societal expectations and legal mandates can create a paradoxical situation for these practitioners. Medical ethics require them to respect a patient's autonomy, including the right to decide whether or not to terminate a pregnancy. However, honoring this choice can be challenging when it involves actively participating in what some view as an ethically fraught decision. Balancing these competing duties demands more than mere clinical judgment; it requires a philosophical inquiry into the nature of duty itself.

For those grounded firmly in their faith, the Catholic doctrine offers a clear perspective. The teachings of the Church have long held that life begins at conception, and abortion is considered a grave moral wrong. A devout medical practitioner is likely to experience intense internal conflict when asked to perform or even assist in an abortion. Their spiritual beliefs may guide them to view each embryo as imbued with divine potential, regardless of the circumstances surrounding conception.

In practice, these dilemmas are not solely personal. They extend into professional realms as well, where practitioners must navigate regulatory frameworks and potential conflicts with colleagues who might hold differing views. Institutional policies and the growing commodification of healthcare often pressure doctors to comply with procedures they might personally abhor. Herein lies another layer of complexity, where physicians might feel compelled to choose between their ethical beliefs and professional survival.

Many have found solace in the concept of conscientious objection, exercising the right to refuse participation in procedures that conflict with their moral or religious beliefs. However, this avenue is not without its challenges. Practitioners who opt for this route must often deal with administrative hurdles, professional repercussions, and, in some cases, scorn from peers and patients alike. They walk a narrow path, maintaining their moral integrity while striving to uphold their roles in the medical community.

The landscape of abortion practices is ever-evolving, and with it, the moral dilemmas faced by medical practitioners. They must remain informed about legal changes and emerging medical technologies, which further complicate the ethical landscape. Advances in prenatal imaging and genetic testing have sparked debates about the moral implications of selective abortion, prompting doctors to reflect on their roles in these deeply personal decisions.

From a historical perspective, medical practitioners have played varied roles in abortion throughout the ages. In ancient times, some healers facilitated abortions to protect the health and well-being of women facing grave circumstances. As society's views on abortion have shifted over the centuries, so too have the ethics and practicalities surrounding medical professionals' involvement. Reflecting on this history provides context for the current ethical challenges and helps practitioners navigate these dilemmas with greater awareness.

For those who struggle with these decisions, support can be found in moral and ethical discourse communities. Engaging with others who share similar dilemmas offers an opportunity to explore and refine personal beliefs within a supportive framework. It also allows for the exchange of experiences and strategies for coping with the emotional toll of such decision-making.

No matter how a practitioner chooses to navigate the moral dilemmas associated with abortion, the decision is deeply personal and often life-altering. They must confront not only the immediate impact on their professional practice, but also the long-term implications for their conscience, spiritual well-being, and professional relationships. Engel and Moore suggest that wrestling with these issues over time can lead to greater self-awareness and professional integrity, providing a clear sense of purpose and philosophical grounding amid the tumult of modern medicine.

Ultimately, the moral dilemmas faced by medical practitioners in the realm of abortion highlight a fundamental tension between professional duties, personal beliefs, and societal expectations. It's a tension that requires careful navigation, empathy, and reflection, underscoring the need for continued dialogue, education, and support within the medical community. Only through such efforts can practitioners hope to reconcile their roles as healers in an area so deeply fraught with moral and ethical complexities.

Chapter 10: Historical Perspectives on Abortion

As we delve into the storied tapestry of history, we find that abortion has cast a prolonged shadow over civilizations through the ages. From ancient practices in Greece and Rome, where philosophers debated the moral implications, to the stern condemnations by medieval theologians, the act of ending a pregnancy has always been fraught with contention. While societies have oscillated between acceptance and rejection, the undercurrents of suffering, experienced by both individuals and the collective conscience, remain a consistent and somber thread. Notably, key historical figures and movements have played pivotal roles in shaping the dialogues that have persisted across centuries, leaving an indelible impact on societal values and ethical norms. This historical lens reveals not just the continuity of conflict but also the silent cries for justice and dignity, imploring those of us today to examine the true cost borne by humanity. In embracing the lessons of history, we are called to unravel the intricate web of deceit that the abortion industry has meticulously woven, advocating for truth, compassion, and a vision of society that honors life in its myriad forms.

Abortion Practices Through the Ages

Throughout history, abortion practices have been deeply embedded in the fabric of human societies, often reflecting the prevailing cultural, moral, and legal attitudes of the time. From antiquity to the modern era, the methods and motivations have evolved, yet the essential questions surrounding the sanctity of life and human dignity remain steadfast. As we explore these practices, it becomes evident that the history of abortion is not merely a history of medical procedures but a testament to the ongoing struggle between preserving life and extinguishing it.

In ancient times, abortion was both a common and controversial practice. Cultures across the world developed various methods, often crude and dangerous, to induce abortion. In ancient Greece, where renowned philosophers like Aristotle considered it a moral option under particular circumstances, various herbal concoctions and physical manipulation methods were employed. Meanwhile, Roman law was more pragmatic, neither explicitly endorsing nor condemning it, leaving the choice largely to the discretion of the head of the family.

The medical knowledge of antiquity, though rudimentary by today's standards, played a significant role in shaping abortion practices. The use of abortifacient herbs such as pennyroyal and silphium was widespread, although their efficacy and safety were a matter of considerable risk. Midwives and healers, often revered and sometimes reviled, were key figures in administering these concoctions, carrying the dual burden of medical practitioner and moral adjudicator.

As we transition to the medieval period, the attitudes towards abortion underwent significant changes, heavily influenced by the rise of Christianity. The Church's influence grew, and a stricter ethic regarding the sanctity of life gained prominence. Canon law began to shape societal views, viewing abortion as a moral failing. This period marked the beginning of a more pervasive sense of ethical opposition to abortion, though practices did persist in the shadows, aided by traditional healing knowledge.

In medieval Europe, belief in the "quickening" — the moment when the mother's perception of fetal movement was thought to signify life — dictated society's legal and moral stance. This concept gave rise to a myriad of beliefs and practices about when a fetus was endowed with life, further complicating the ethical landscape and reflecting the region's burgeoning religiosity contrasted by persistent folk practices.

With the onset of the Renaissance and the Enlightenment, scientific exploration began pushing the boundaries of knowledge, including reproductive health. This era saw burgeoning debates on the nature of humanity and the moral implications of abortion. Legal frameworks still largely frowned upon the practice, yet societal whispers of its continued occurrence persisted, adapting to the nascent medical methodologies emerging at the time.

The Enlightenment introduced the notion that individual reason should guide moral choices, influencing some to argue for a more liberal approach to abortion. Paradoxically, this period also saw an increased effort to criminalize the practice in many European countries, where the state and church often worked in tandem to preserve social order and morals, shaping laws through a lens of preserving societal sanctity rather than individual choice.

The 19th century brought technological and medical advances, along with an era of burgeoning industrial societies, where abortion began to be more overtly discussed and challenged. The development of more precise surgical techniques introduced new possibilities, albeit with significant risks. Industrialization's socio-economic challenges, such as urban poverty and overcrowding, often led women to seek abortions out of desperation.

Towards the late 19th and early 20th centuries, as advancing medical technologies and emerging feminist movements intersected, the discourse around abortion began to transform radically. Women's rights advocates started framing the discussion around bodily autonomy and gender rights, challenging traditional norms and advocating for legal and medical recognition of their reproductive choices. This spurred intense debates throughout the 20th century over who had the right to decide the fate of unborn life.

In the mid-20th century, abortion became a flashpoint in cultural and legal battlegrounds across the world, evolving from clandestine operations to courtrooms and public squares. Countries diverged in their approaches, with some adopting more liberal policies while others clung to conservative values. During this period, the medicalization of abortion improved safety but did not quell the ethical storm surrounding it.

Technological advancements in the latter half of the 20th century, including ultrasound and improved surgical methods, altered the scope and perception of abortion once more. These technologies provided new insights into fetal development, complicating the ethical landscape further and heralding an age where medical facts often clashed with personal beliefs and legal precedents.

As we step into the 21st century, the evolution of abortion practices is marked by both technological sophistication and deeply entrenched ethical divisions. The so-called 'abortion pill' made its way into the narrative, introducing medical abortion as a widespread method, riddled with its own set of scientific, moral, and legal challenges.

Our exploration of abortion practices through the ages reveals a complex tapestry of human endeavor. It showcases the tensions between life, autonomy, authority, and the quest for moral clarity. In today's world, where abortion remains a polarizing topic, understanding its historical context is vital. It's not just about realizing the technological progress but recognizing the enduring ethical dilemmas and societal impacts that have shadowed this practice for centuries. We are called to discern the paths that sustain life, dignity, and hope in the continuum of human history.

Key Historical Figures and Movements

Throughout history, significant individuals and movements have shaped the dialogue and perspectives on abortion, often navigating the tumultuous waters of socio-political change and moral debate. These narratives provide a lens through which we can examine how abortion has been perceived and contested in various epochs.

One of the earliest recorded figures in the discussion of abortion was Hippocrates, the ancient Greek physician known for the Hippocratic Oath. Although interpretations of the oath vary, its commitment to "do no harm" laid early foundations for medical ethics, impacting how abortion was viewed in medical practice. The oath's ambiguous stance left room for interpretation, contributing to a historical continuum of debate about the morals and duties of physicians when it comes to the life of the unborn.

The Middle Ages in Europe marked a time of significant influence from religious figures, notably St. Thomas Aquinas, whose writings continue to echo through modern theological debates. He tackled profound questions of human existence and morality, suggesting that life began at "ensoulment," a point that stirred much debate. Aquinas' influence has echoed down the ages, forming a cornerstone of Catholic doctrine. His interpretations of the beginning of life continue to underpin the Church's pro-life stance, a position still fervently debated and upheld within modern Catholic circles.

Moving forward into the Enlightenment, the era brought about a renaissance in human rights thinking. Mary Wollstonecraft, an English writer and philosopher, became an early proponent of women's rights. Though not directly addressing abortion, her advocacy for women's autonomy in educational and personal realms questioned the societal roles imposed on women, nudging forward the conversation about reproductive rights and the broader context in which they are situated. Her influence laid groundwork for future feminist discourse, intertwining the ongoing struggle for women's rights with the ethical and moral dimensions of abortion.

The 19th and early 20th centuries saw the rise of movements directly challenging abortion on ethical grounds. Figures like Dr. Horatio Storer led campaigns against abortion in the United States. The Storer movement, part of a medical model promoting the notion that abortion was criminal, facilitated the adoption of restrictive laws across multiple states. These efforts established a framework that would dominate the legal landscape of abortion until the latter half of the 20th century, adding a legal dimension to the ethical fight.

The post-World War II era marked a pivotal shift with the burgeoning feminist movements, highlighted by figures such as Margaret Sanger. Though highly controversial due to her association with eugenic ideologies, Sanger's advocacy for birth control was instrumental in shaping the discourse surrounding women's access to reproductive health. Her work paved the way for the introduction and broader acceptance of modern contraceptive methods, contributing indirectly to the evolving conversation about reproductive choice and abortion.

As the 20th century progressed into the 1960s and 1970s, landmark figures like Dr. Bernard Nathanson emerged from within the abortion rights movement, actively participating in its early developments. However, his later conversion into a fierce pro-life advocate after witnessing ultrasound images of unborn fetuses was a significant turning point. His shift highlighted the profound personal and ethical dilemmas posed by abortion and brought to the fore the potential of medical technology to influence public sentiment and personal convictions on the matter.

Parallel to individual figures, various movements arose, altering the landscape of abortion discourse globally. The pro-life movement gained momentum, drawing support from religious organizations and conservative political groups. Countless individuals, galvanized by faith and moral conviction, joined hands to advocate for policies that protect the rights of the unborn. Conferences, marches, and peaceful protests became symbolic of a collective endeavor to enact legal protections and provide support systems for expectant mothers.

On the opposing front, the pro-choice movement emerged, bolstered by a coalition of feminists, healthcare professionals, and human rights advocates. This collective fought for what they viewed as women's inalienable right to autonomy over their own bodies. The movement openly challenged restrictive abortion laws, spearheading campaigns that emphasized personal choice and secular values. This divergence of ideology birthed public debate that pervades political arenas and social discourse to this day.

The complex interplay between these individuals and movements has shaped the global narrative surrounding abortion, fostering a spectrum of perspectives informed by diverse cultural backdrops. In examining the profound impact of historical figures and movements in this light, we are reminded of the multifaceted nature of the abortion debate—one where moral, ethical, and personal dimensions intertwine.

These dialogues invite reflection on how the echoes of the past inform our current understanding and legislation. They present an opportunity for communities, particularly within the Roman Catholic tradition, to engage thoughtfully with the issue while navigating the challenge of rendering compassionate and informed ethical judgments. As we continue forward, understanding history's weight on such a critical issue is vital. It not only influences the strategies and conversations of today but also uplifts the voices of those who have, throughout time, sought to share truth in their pursuit of what they believed to be in the service of justice and human dignity.

Chapter 11: The Role of Media in Shaping Abortion Views

The profound power of media in molding public perception of abortion can't be underestimated. As narratives woven through news outlets, films, and social media permeate society, they often shape the collective consciousness in ways visible and unseen. Within this intricate dance of information, bias frequently masquerades as truth, subtly influencing opinions and swaying beliefs. The media's portrayal can paint abortion with the broad strokes of personal choice, omitting the nuanced agony of moral and ethical conflict that many experience. This creates a dystopian reality where complexity is masked by simplicity and genuine human suffering is reduced to soundbites. It's imperative to discern the media's role in this dialogue, recognizing how it might amplify certain voices while silencing others, thus leading society down a path that detaches from authentic human experience and ethical reflection.

Analyzing Media Bias

In a world increasingly saturated by a multitude of media channels, understanding the narratives presented by these platforms is crucial for grasping how public opinions, especially on sensitive topics like abortion, are shaped. The media, with its pervasive influence, often acts as both a mirror and a molder of societal beliefs, creating ripples that extend far beyond any single broadcast or publication. This dynamic interplay between media messaging and audience perception becomes particularly potent when exploring the narratives around abortion.

Media bias can subtly, or not so subtly, skew perceptions by controlling the narrative's emphasis, language, and context. It often operates in the shadows, undetected yet profoundly impactful. The portrayal of the abortion debate within media outlets either demonizes or canonizes the entities involved, crafting a story that aligns with their ideological leanings. Rarely neutral, this portrayal often molds societal divisions, cementing ideologies with evocative imagery and emotionally charged terminology.

Consider how the framing of abortion protesters varies between networks. Some are depicted as standing defiantly in defense of women's autonomy while others are portrayed as vociferously championing the sanctity of life. This dichotomy, fueled by the adjectives and descriptors employed, can subtly prod audiences towards predetermined conclusions, without their conscious realization.

Yet, the insight extends deeper. The selection of spokespeople, experts, and subjects interviewed can create an echo chamber effect, reinforcing pre-existing biases. Media outlets often choose individuals who represent the extremes of the debate, rather than those who can provide balanced or nuanced perspectives. This sensationalism draws eye-catching headlines and fosters emotional engagement but offers little in terms of genuine understanding.

In recent decades, the role of media in shaping public consciousness has expanded exponentially with the rise of digital platforms. Online articles, social media debates, and viral content share the stage with traditional media, each contributing to the rapidly evolving narrative tapestry. Here, algorithms play a significant role, determining what content is shown to whom, often based on past engagement rather than objectivity. This algorithm-driven curation heightens the effects of media bias, tailoring experiences to reinforce users' preexisting beliefs.

In such an environment, critical thinking becomes more essential than ever. Misinterpretations, half-truths, and outright falsehoods can masquerade as reputable information, influencing decision-making and societal views. While media bias is an almost inevitable reality when presenting complex issues, a discerning audience equipped with the tools for critical analysis can pierce through the narrative layers to uncover a more balanced understanding.

Nevertheless, the task remains daunting for many. Media literacy education, then, becomes a vital component in combating the inherent biases within media ecosystems. By understanding and identifying bias, individuals can better navigate the labyrinth of narratives they face, forging paths onto solid ground amidst swirling uncertainties. In this endeavor, communities, educational institutions, and faith organizations hold a pivotal role in equipping their members with the skills necessary to discern truth amidst conflicting reports.

As we dissect the media's influence in shaping abortion views, it is imperative that we maintain an awareness of the distinct yet interconnected elements that form this complex web. The choice of language, imagery, and contextual background all contribute to the subliminal currents that guide societal perspectives. With careful observation, one can illuminate these currents and, perhaps, reshape them towards a more just and truthful representation of reality.

Furthermore, historical analysis highlights that over time, media presentations of abortion reflect broader societal shifts. From stigmatization to normalization, from back-alley procedures to discussions of reproductive rights, the portrayal within media has mirrored and influenced cultural attitudes towards abortion. In this dance of influencing and being influenced, media bias stands as both an artifact and architect of the abortion discourse.

In aligning with a proactive stance against biased rhetoric, it becomes essential to cultivate forums for diverse voices and experiences. This diversification allows for a more comprehensive, empathetic portrayal of the multidimensional abortion narrative. By promoting a spectrum of stories, the media can better educate its audiences, steering them towards informed and compassionate viewpoints.

This analysis of media bias calls upon each reader to question, to probe, to dialogue with both the information presented and with each other, striving to discern beneath the surface. The path may not always be clear, and opinions will inevitably vary. Nevertheless, through committed pursuit and open-minded engagement, media bias in abortion discourse can be recognized, critiqued, and, ultimately, transcended, paving the way for more authentic conversations and societal healing.

In conclusion, the role of media in shaping abortion views is both pivotal and complex. By shedding light on how bias operates within this domain, we take a critical step towards fostering a more informed and nuanced public understanding of abortion. The hope remains that through conscious engagement with media content, society might progress towards a future where discourse is anchored in truthfulness and compassion.

Influence of Propaganda on Public Opinion

In a world where words and images flash before our eyes every waking moment, propaganda is an insidious force shaping public opinion on abortion. The media, wielding immense power over hearts and minds, often disseminates carefully tailored messages that influence perceptions and decisions. The goal of much of this propaganda is not simply to inform but to persuade—to mold public sentiment and align it with specific agendas.

Propaganda, by its very nature, thrives on repetition and simplicity. In the context of abortion, it repeatedly delivers narratives and images designed to evoke strong emotional responses, whether through crafted news segments, opinion pieces, or social media campaigns. These messages can oversimplify complex issues, reducing them to binary choices and emotionally charged slogans. This approach dismisses the nuances necessary for a well-informed public discourse and leads individuals to adopt views without fully understanding the implications of their beliefs.

Propagandistic strategies often exploit the natural emotions surrounding abortion—emotions of hope, fear, and morality. For instance, in many cases, the media employs images that dehumanize or depersonalize the unborn, portraying them in abstract terms such as "clumps of cells." Conversely, some narratives use imagery of vulnerable women, emphasizing personal autonomy and choice without addressing the deeper ethical and societal consequences of abortion. Such strategies can skew perceptions, suggesting that the issue is merely a matter of personal freedom, forgetting the moral and communal dimensions.

Central to the effectiveness of propaganda is its ability to create echo chambers where only like-minded opinions are amplified, and dissenting voices are marginalized or silenced. This isolation of ideas can be particularly damaging among communities where religious and moral considerations are pivotal, such as within the Roman Catholic community. Here, propaganda might either challenge traditional beliefs or attempt to reinforce them in ways that polarize rather than unite believers.

The Catholic Church, with its longstanding teachings on the sanctity of life, often finds itself countering propagandistic narratives that undermine its doctrine. In doing so, it emphasizes the importance of truth, dignity, and respect for all human life. The Church calls for a deeper reflection on the moral implications of accepting the narratives promoted by the abortion industry, urging individuals to resist the oversimplifications offered by mainstream propaganda.

Chesterton's wisdom reminds us that in the face of dominant narratives, individuals must hold fast to reason and truth. In this light, media literacy becomes crucial for those wishing to understand the true nature of abortion advocacy and its societal implications. By cultivating critical thinking skills, people can discern between propagandistic messages and truthful reporting. Aquinas would argue that a society grounded in truth must seek the good of all its members, both born and unborn, and reject messages that clash with the inherent dignity of human life.

When propaganda goes unchecked, it can lead to a society that views moral truths as relative rather than absolute. This jeopardizes the very foundation of human values cherished across generations. The utopian vision of a society grounded in authentic human dignity becomes a dystopian reality when lies and half-truths about abortion prevail. Unchallenged propaganda contributes to a culture where expediency trumps ethical considerations.

The challenge, then, is to expose the lies of abortion propaganda and encourage a return to genuine human values, where life is affirmed, and society's weakest are protected. It requires an understanding that true freedom doesn't mean choosing without consequence but rather making decisions aligned with truth and goodness. This perspective invites a reevaluation of the role of the media and its responsibility to the public.

A key consideration for pregnant mothers, historians, and Roman Catholics alike is the recognition that media often operates out of sight, shaping narratives subtly and pervasively. Pregnant women are particularly vulnerable to media influences, as they may find themselves pressured by prevailing cultural narratives rather than being supported in choices that affirm life. Historians must understand how propaganda has historically shaped public opinion and policy, often at the expense of ethical standards.

Ultimately, combating propaganda requires a communal effort to uphold the sanctity of life. This involves advocating for media systems that promote dialogue rather than division, education rather than manipulation, and respect rather than exploitation. Engaging in constructive conversation allows for a diverse range of voices and ensures that the truth about abortion and its impact on women, families, and society is heard.

In the spirit of Pope Saint John Paul II, let us strive for a civilization of love, where the truths of the human person are respected, and the dignity of life is upheld. It's a call to transform media from a tool of division into a means of cultivating authentic understanding and compassion. By challenging propaganda, we illuminate the path toward a society where truth reigns, and life, in all its stages, is cherished.

Chapter 12: Pro-Life vs. Pro-Choice Movements

The clash between the pro-life and pro-choice movements stands at the heart of the abortion debate, illustrating a fundamental divergence in how society perceives life and autonomy. The pro-life movement, rooted in the conviction that life begins at conception, champions the protection of the unborn as an unwavering moral imperative, emphasizing compassion and insisting on the inherent dignity of every human being. Meanwhile, the pro-choice advocates argue for reproductive rights, focusing on a woman's autonomy and freedom to make decisions about her own body without external imposition. This battle isn't merely political; it's a deep moral tug-of-war that reflects broader societal values and affects perceptions of family and community. As both sides continue to evolve, incorporating modern philosophical and ethical arguments, the conversation grows ever more intricate and emotionally charged, underscoring the urgent need for mutual understanding and dialogue that transcends slogans and sound bites.

Founding and Evolution of Pro-Life Advocacy

The roots of the pro-life advocacy movement can be traced back to the inherent belief in the sanctity of life, a principle deeply embedded within the moral frameworks of numerous religious and cultural traditions. Embodying these values, the early advocates for life focused their energies on disseminating awareness and galvanizing the masses, speaking out against the practice of abortion as an affront to the dignity of human life. This conviction is not merely a philosophical discourse but a call to action, a moral imperative that beckons both individuals and institutions to stand as guardians of the defenseless.

In the mid-20th century, as medical practices evolved and legal frameworks reshaped the landscape of reproductive rights, the pro-life movement gained momentum. This period was marked by a recognizably dystopian shift in societal norms, where the sanctity of life was frequently overshadowed by a burgeoning emphasis on personal autonomy. However, this backdrop also became a fertile ground for the rise of organized pro-life advocacy. One pivotal moment was the watershed year of 1973, when Roe v. Wade profoundly altered the legal and cultural dialogue around abortion in the United States. In response, various groups sprang into action, determined to challenge and counteract the narrative that abortion was merely a matter of individual choice.

Efforts intensified to educate the public about the realities of abortion and its impact on both the individual and society. Pro-life advocates utilized various platforms to disseminate their message, highlighting the devastating physical, emotional, and spiritual toll abortion often precipitates. They also worked tirelessly to expose the hidden agendas within the abortion industry, painting it as a mechanical process that undermines the fundamental values of life and family. Their mission was not just reactive but deeply rooted in a keen awareness of human dignity, much in line with the teachings found in many moral and religious doctrines, emphasizing the interconnectedness of all life.

Around the same time, significant figures began to emerge, galvanizing communities and reinforcing the philosophical tenets of the pro-life cause. These leaders, often grounded in religious traditions, summoned the courage to speak against societal trends, laying a foundation that the movement would build upon. Organizations were formed, such as the National Right to Life Committee, which coordinated grass-roots efforts across states and set the stage for national debates and policy discussions. Their role was crucial in transforming isolated voices into a cohesive narrative that championed the preservation of life at every possible juncture.

The evolution of the pro-life advocacy movement also saw a remarkable synthesis of moral reasoning and scientific advancement. As technology provided a clearer window into the womb, revealing the intricacies of fetal development, pro-life advocates harnessed this knowledge to bolster their case. Ultrasound images served not only as scientific evidence but as poignant reminders of the humanity residing within the unborn. This led to a robust dialogue about fetal rights that challenged perceptions and added complexity to the moral discourse surrounding abortion. The convergence of faith and reason became a pivotal characteristic of the movement, echoing a utopian vision where science and ethics are not adversaries but allies in the quest to affirm life.

One can't overlook the international dimension of the movement's evolution. Pro-life advocacy is not confined by borders; its principles resonate globally, finding allies in communities across continents. International coalitions and partnerships have emerged, sharing strategies, resources, and successes to act against abortion's pervasive reach. In many regions, this has led to legal reforms and societal shifts, reflecting a growing recognition of the movement's influence and the enduring strength of its message.

Over the decades, the movement has diversified and adapted to overcome challenges posed by the shifting socio-political environment. This adaptability is evident in their embrace of various forms of media and communication to reach wider audiences. Social media, documentaries, and public campaigns have become critical tools for advocacy, enabling real-time engagement and mobilization. By leveraging these platforms, pro-life advocates have reinvigorated the conversation around life's sanctity, ensuring that their message remains relevant and influential in contemporary discourse.

It is essential to acknowledge that the journey of pro-life advocacy has not been without conflict or criticism. Navigating the polarizing landscape of abortion politics, pro-life advocates have often faced accusations of impeding personal freedom or infringing on women's rights. Nonetheless, they maintain that true freedom is deeply entwined with the respect for life, insisting upon the protection of the most vulnerable as a moral duty. In doing so, they continually engage with complex ethical questions, reflecting a commitment to fostering a culture of life that transcends political rhetoric.

This ongoing evolution showcases a remarkable tenacity and resolve, continuously seeking ways to better articulate and defend the pro-life position. Whether through legislation, education, or compassionate service, the movement demonstrates a profound dedication to its core belief—that life, in all its forms, is precious and worthy of protection. It seeks not only to oppose abortion but to offer alternatives, such as adoption, furthering the dialogue on supporting mothers and families in making life-affirming decisions.

Thus, as the movement advances and new challenges emerge, pro-life advocacy remains a potent force within the broader socio-cultural landscape. Its growth is a testament to the enduring power of a united vision rooted in compassion, reason, and an unwavering commitment to uphold life. By adapting to contemporary needs and asserting its relevance in modern debates, the movement continues to aspire towards a more compassionate society, where every life is cherished and protected. This evolution, etched into the annals of history, serves as a beacon of hope for the future, urging society to reflect deeply on the values it holds dear and the legacy it wishes to leave behind.

Examination of Pro-Choice Arguments

The pro-choice movement, animated by the principle of bodily autonomy, has presented a slew of arguments that resonate with many in modern society. Rooted in the belief that women should have the authority to make decisions concerning their own bodies, these arguments are both fervent and multifaceted. However, upon closer examination, the purported empowerment offered by the pro-choice narrative can often occlude the deeper implications for the individual, family, and society at large.

One mainstay of pro-choice reasoning revolves around the concept of personal liberty. Advocates argue that denying a woman the right to terminate a pregnancy infringes upon her personal freedom and self-determination. It's a compelling argument at first glance. The idea that women should control their reproductive futures aligns with broader societal shifts toward individual rights. Yet, when we delve deeper, does this freedom always lead to empowerment, or is it potentially an illusion that overlooks the emotional and psychological repercussions that often follow an abortion? This freedom, while celebrated, can sometimes manifest as a heavy burden of choice.

Another cornerstone of pro-choice rhetoric is the emphasis on "safe, legal, and rare" abortions. The assumption here is that by ensuring legal access, the safety of procedures improves and the incidence decreases. Pro-choice advocates often herald the legalization of abortion as a triumph over the grim specter of dangerous, clandestine procedures. While there's no denying that legality can correlate with safety, do we overlook the inherent risks and long-term consequences that still accompany these "safe" procedures?

Economic factors also heavily weigh in the discussion. Many pro-choice arguments highlight the financial implications of carrying an unwanted pregnancy to term. They argue that forcing a woman to bear a child for which she is unprepared or unable to care financially is an undue burden that exacerbates cycles of poverty. Yet, can we ignore the larger economic narrative? The long-term social costs that ripple through generations outstrip the immediate financial relief that abortion might provide.

The language used by pro-choice advocates often frames the debate in terms of health. They emphasize the idea that abortion is a healthcare necessity, crucial for protecting women in cases where their health might be compromised. However, statistics reveal that abortions performed for health reasons form a small fraction of total procedures. When health becomes a mask for broader motives, we risk diminishing the gravity of genuine medical emergencies, stretching the truth to fit a more palatable argument.

Notably, the pro-choice movement positions itself as a counterpoint to perceived patriarchal structures. The claim is that opposition to abortion is a thin veneer for controlling women's reproductive rights. While acknowledging the unfortunate historical contexts that validate such concerns, does circular reasoning sometimes undermine the complexity and diversity of pro-life voices, many of which include women advocating out of compassion and genuine concern?

A persuasive yet contentious pro-choice argument is the assertion that a fetus does not hold moral status and thus does not possess rights equivalent to those of a born person. Proponents argue that a fetus's dependency on the mother negates its autonomy and individuality, justifying its termination. This view, however, invites deeper philosophical considerations about life's sanctity and at what point potentiality converts to actuality. Can we afford to dismiss these ethical nuances in favor of convenience?

Beneath all these arguments lies a profound existential question: What are the cumulative effects of a society that normalizes abortion? While pro-choice advocates may not overtly address this, the implications are clear. If life's beginning is subject to personal interpretation, can this lead to a societal desensitization towards life itself? A broader examination might reveal unforeseen impacts on human values and collective consciousness.

Furthermore, the societal support—or lack thereof—available to women facing unplanned pregnancies factors prominently in pro-choice discourse. The narrative often implies that without access to abortion, women are left isolated and unsupported. While this highlights genuine gaps in societal support structures, it sidesteps the essential question: Shouldn't efforts converge on strengthening these structures rather than curtailing life?

It's also crucial to consider the intersection of pro-choice arguments with issues of race and class. The abortion debate is inextricably linked to larger conversations about inequality, as pro-choice advocates point out the disparate impact on marginalized communities. Yet, there's a haunting undercurrent: Are we inadvertently perpetuating discriminatory practices that undervalue certain lives by promoting abortion as a solution to systemic inequities?

Ultimately, the pro-choice stance encapsulates a spectrum of human experiences and emotions. It seeks to address real fears and vulnerabilities but often with simplistic solutions to complex problems. A nuanced examination suggests that, while the arguments seem empowering, they sometimes neglect to fully address the broader societal implications and moral considerations that make this issue profoundly intricate. As we navigate this discussion, we must question whether we are trading temporary autonomy for long-term societal erosion.

Chapter 13: Case Studies in Abortion Tragedies

Caught in society's web of promises and deceptions, many who have walked the path of abortion find themselves grappling with profound loss and regret—a reality that tells tales beyond the cold statistics. These case studies unveil personal tragedies, each narrative echoing the desolation of potential unfulfilled and lives altered irreversibly. For some, the decision led to a haunting void, an absence marked not only by physical loss but by emotional and spiritual scars that time struggles to heal. The tragic alignment of cultural pressures and personal desperation uncovers a dystopian landscape where the sanctity of life is overshadowed by false freedoms. Such stories are not hushed whispers of the past but loud reminders of the pivotal need for change, for they reveal the chasms in humanity's moral fabric. The lessons gleaned from these tragedies remind us of the inherent value of life and the critical role compassion and truth must play in guiding women and society towards more hopeful choices. As we delve into their stories, we recognize abortion's ripple effect, weaving destruction into the very tapestry of familial and societal bonds we strive to uphold.

Personal Stories of Loss and Regret

In the quiet aftermath of an abortion, many women find themselves wrestling with an overwhelming array of emotions. The promise of relief so often touted by proponents of the procedure is eclipsed by a deep, often unnameable sorrow. It is in these untold stories where the real tragedies unfold, both in the lives of those directly involved and in the ripple effects felt within their families and communities.

Consider the story of Maria, a young woman full of aspirations and dreams. She had plans to pursue her education and make her mark on the world. When she discovered she was pregnant, panic quickly set in. The voices around her were insistent—some well-meaning, others not—that an abortion was the sensible path. In a haze of anxiety and desperation, she went through with it, convinced it was the only way to preserve her future. Yet in the silence that followed, Maria was left with a profound sense of loss, a shadow that lingered and grew as the months and years went by.

Maria's experience was more than just her own; it was shared by those around her. Her family, though outwardly supportive at first, found themselves splintering under the weight of an unspoken grief. The future she had envisioned felt forever altered, not only by the absence of the child she once carried but by the fracture in her own heart.

Then there's James and Emily, a couple who faced an impossible situation. With financial struggles already straining their relationship, a pregnancy brought an unwelcome complexity. They were led to believe that ending the pregnancy was a solution. Emily felt relief, but it was short-lived. The delicate fabric of their relationship, once strong enough to withstand external pressures, slowly unraveled under the burden of unacknowledged grief. The intimacy they once enjoyed became clouded by a pervasive sense of regret.

Such stories are not rare, unfortunately; they echo across communities, affect countless people, and reverberate through time. The wounds inflicted are not merely emotional or psychological. They cut deeply, influencing decisions and relationships, and sometimes, the course of a lifetime.

In contrast, Maggie's narrative is one of a slow, pervasive healing process. After falling into a deep well of regret post-abortion, she discovered a path not only towards forgiveness but towards an understanding of herself as well. Her healing journey involved community support, reassurance from her faith, and a gradual acceptance of her loss. This transformation didn't erase the pain but allowed her to rise above it, redefining what her future could look like, albeit a future different from what she had planned.

These personal tales underscore the multifaceted tragedy of abortion and its often understated personal toll. They offer a poignant reminder of what is at stake—not just one life, but the interconnected web of lives touched by each decision.

The choices made in those moments are theirs alone, yet the societal structures, narratives, and pressures that inform them are familiar to countless others. These stories illuminate the need for a more compassionate understanding and discourse about life's sanctity, and the real, human cost when it is disregarded. They remind us of the inherent dignity of every person and the irreparable emptiness that follows the denial of that dignity.

Through these narratives of loss and regret, we are called to not only acknowledge the profound impact of abortion on individuals but also to question the societal norms that so readily accept it as an unchallenged option. In doing so, we create space for change—a chance to heal, and an opportunity to prevent future tragedies.

Societal Lessons Learned

In the midst of the complexities surrounding abortion, pivotal societal lessons emerge, woven intricately into the tapestry of communities and cultures. The stories of individual tragedies, as discussed in the case studies, underscore a collective awakening to the profound consequences abortion has on society at large. These stories act as reflections in a grand societal mirror, challenging us to question how we got here and where we are headed.

Historically, societies have grappled with abortion, revealing the stark contrasts in how different cultures approach this contentious issue. Each case of tragedy paints a broader picture, illustrating how societies either succumb to the normalization of abortion or resist it by advocating for life with vigor and compassion. The lessons learned from these case studies remind us that the societal psyche is continuously shaped by the decisions surrounding abortion.

The erosion of familial structures and values stands as one of the most striking lessons. When the sanctity of life is compromised at any stage, the foundational beliefs that hold families together begin to waver. Families find themselves struggling to reconcile the loss of potential futures, of generations unborn. This disruption leads to an altered perception of kinship and the intrinsic value of familial bonds.

As societies increasingly entertain the concept of abortion as a right rather than a loss, a second societal lesson emerges: the impact on social empathy. Case studies highlight a growing desensitization towards the suffering of others, including those whose lives are lost before they even begin. This erosion of empathy manifests in various aspects, from the media's portrayal of abortion to individual interactions within communities. In valuing convenience over compassion, society risks becoming unmoored from its humanities.

A closer examination of these tragedies also reveals significant economic repercussions. While abortion is often couched in economic terms—

suggesting relief from financial burdens—the long-term economic consequences tell a different story. Societies face the challenge of sustaining dwindling populations, leading to potential labor shortages and economic stagnation. Such revelations compel us to rethink the immediate economic rationale behind abortion and scrutinize its societal costs more deeply.

Moreover, societal lessons extend into the realm of ethical and moral questioning. Abortion compels us to engage in a dialogue about human rights, stretching the fabric of legality and morality. The right to life versus the right to choose creates a landscape where moral imperatives often clash with legal frameworks. This discordance invites profound reflection on the ethical responsibilities we hold towards both the born and the unborn.

Inextricably linked to these moral dilemmas is the role of education and awareness. A society's collective conscience evolves through what it learns and unlearns, and the stories of abortion tragedies significantly influence this process. The exposure to real-life consequences encourages educational systems and organizations to invest in comprehensive awareness campaigns, which aim to equip young minds with the knowledge to make informed decisions.

Furthermore, the societal lessons stretch into the realm of health care. The repercussions on women's health, both physical and mental, emphasize the need for a more nuanced understanding of abortion's impact. The tragedies underline the importance of medical professionals being better equipped to support women holistically, beyond mere physical procedures. This extends to mental health support, ensuring no woman silently bears the weight of decision alone.

Lessons also teach us to reconsider community and faith-based support structures. With the growing recognition of abortion's long-term effects, we witness communities coming together to offer solace, healing, and alternatives. These systems reinforce the idea that no individual should ever feel isolated in making or living through such a significant choice. They foster a culture of empathy and understanding, essential for societal cohesion.

Significantly, these societal lessons challenge us to rethink our advocacy strategies. The stories within case studies become powerful tools for promoting life-affirming cultures. They urge advocacy groups to harness the emotional resonance of these narratives to energize campaigns for change and support legislative efforts that respect and uphold the sanctity of life.

In conclusion, the lessons learned from case studies in abortion tragedies are vast and profound. They compel us as a society to reflect deeply on our values, re-evaluate our choices, and reignite our commitment to life and love. In doing so, we not only learn from past tragedies but equip ourselves to foster a future where every human life is regarded with dignity and reverence.

Chapter 14: Global Perspectives on Abortion

As we turn our gaze to the global stage, the varied landscape of abortion laws and attitudes lays bare a tapestry of contrasts that reflect the deep-rooted values and historical trajectories of different nations. In countries where traditions intertwine with stringent laws, such as Poland or El Salvador, the sanctity of life stands as a sacrosanct principle, shaping societal norms and personal beliefs. Meanwhile, nations like Canada and the Netherlands adopt an approach that favors autonomy and the perceived rights of choice. Cross-cultural attitudes towards abortion are often enmeshed with economic and social factors, leaving an indelible mark on familial structures and communal relationships. The global discourse, therefore, oscillates between advocating for personal agency and recognizing the inherent value of unborn life, highlighting a profound ethical tension that binds humanity in its quest for moral clarity. In each country's legal framework, one can see the reflection of its values—sometimes creating a utopian vision of harmony, while at other times revealing dystopian realities of division and discord.

Abortion Laws Around the World

Across the globe, abortion laws reflect a tapestry of cultural, social, and moral beliefs. Each nation, with its unique historical and ethical context, offers a distinct perspective on the legality and accessibility of abortion. From stringent laws to liberal approaches, this diversity reveals not just geographical differences but also profound philosophical divides.

In some countries, such as the United States, the legal landscape is a patchwork where individual states hold sway over abortion policies, leading to varying access levels based on geographical location. The consequences of such heterogeneity can be both divisive and illuminating. On one hand, it showcases the deeply personal nature of abortion debates; on the other, it can lead to disparities in health care and access, where the ability of a woman to exercise her rights depends largely on her zip code. The U.S. is not alone in such divergence. Federal systems, whether found in Australia or Germany, often face similar complexities.

Meanwhile, across the Atlantic in Europe, the approach is more cohesive, yet still varies widely. Some countries like Ireland and Poland showcase a strong influence of religious doctrines reflected in their laws. In Ireland, the legacy of stringent anti-abortion laws has only recently shifted toward slightly more permissive policies following intense public discourse and referendums. In contrast, nations like France and the Netherlands offer a more liberal stance, where abortion is both legally sanctioned and publicly funded.

South America currently stands as a battleground for abortion rights, with countries like Argentina making headlines recently after a hard-fought battle to legalize abortion up to 14 weeks of pregnancy. Such moves represent seismic shifts in a region where Catholic influence is substantial and often inscribed into the laws of the land. Yet, within a short geographical space, countries such as Brazil maintain highly restrictive laws, allowing abortion only in cases of rape, risk to the mother's life, or severe fetal malformations.

A look at Africa reveals a contrasting picture. Here, the debate often transcends health and enters corridors of morality and cultural tradition. Countries like South Africa stand out with some of the most progressive abortion laws on the continent, akin to Western nations in their permissiveness. Meanwhile, many neighboring countries adhere to stringent restrictions that can put both women and health care providers at significant legal risk. These differences often correlate strongly with levels of education and socio-economic development, highlighting the broader societal inequalities that impact women's reproductive rights.

In places like the Middle East and parts of Asia, governmental and religious stances can heavily influence abortion laws. For instance, Iran and Saudi Arabia tightly regulate abortion, primarily permitting it to save the mother's life. These regulations often stem from long-standing cultural and religious beliefs, intertwining with legal codes often difficult for some to challenge. Yet, contrasting pictures emerge within the region, with countries like Israel taking a more liberal approach, where abortion is permitted under various circumstances with committee review.

In Asia, the diversity in abortion laws offers a fascinating contrast. On one end, China has a history of state-controlled reproductive policies, though recent shifts aim to loosen these controls. On the other, Japan allows abortion within a legal framework that includes reasons like economic hardship, reflecting a practical, albeit restrained, approach. Across the continent, in India, abortion is legal on broad grounds, yet accessibility and societal stigma often create barriers, showcasing the gap between policy and practice.

Such global disparities raise ethical questions about autonomy, human rights, and the role of state intervention. Are laws a reflection of societal values, or do they lag behind cultural progression? The answer, as complex and varied as the laws themselves, is far from uncomplicated. What remains clear is the need for ongoing discourse—a conversation that acknowledges past lessons while considering future implications.

These differences in legislation showcase how abortion is more than a medical procedure; it is a reflection of societal values. To expose the so-called lies surrounding the abortion debate, one must first navigate through this complex web of legal variances. We see nations either embracing or rejecting infrastructures of care, empathy, and rights, thereby wielding profound influence on women, the family unit, and society at large.

Legal permissibility does not equate to accessibility. Even in regions with liberal laws, societal stigma or inadequate healthcare infrastructures pose significant barriers. Many women still face logistical and personal challenges when seeking abortions, which further complicates the ethical and practical landscape of reproductive rights. It's a pervasive issue where legality subtly intersects with moral and ideological notions of right and wrong.

As observers of these varied landscapes, we must dive deeper into understanding these legal nuances, for they hold a mirror to society's values and priorities. It's an intricate dance that stands as a testament to humanity's grappling with morality, freedom, and responsibility. Each law, each regulation, is a chapter in an ongoing story—a narrative where the stakes involve not only lives but principles that societies hold close to their core.

Cross-Cultural Attitudes

The tapestry of humanity is woven from diverse cultural threads, each carrying its own beliefs, traditions, and views on numerous aspects of life, including the contentious issue of abortion. Cross-cultural attitudes toward abortion reveal deep-seated values and societal norms that vary widely around the globe. In some regions, this practice is embraced, defended, and seen as a fundamental right, while in others, it is viewed as a grave affront to moral and ethical principles. Navigating these complex landscapes requires an understanding of the cultural nuances that fuel the global conversation on abortion.

In more secular and liberal societies, such as those in Western Europe, abortion is often framed within the context of women's rights, autonomy, and personal choice. Countries like the Netherlands and Sweden exemplify this liberal perspective, providing widespread access to abortion services within their healthcare systems. Their views are heavily influenced by a belief in personal freedom and a separation of religious doctrine from state affairs. This attitude reflects a broader cultural narrative that prioritizes individual rights over communal or religious mores. It creates an environment where the decision to abort is often perceived as a private matter, not subject to public moral scrutiny.

Conversely, in predominantly religious or traditional societies, abortion often faces strong opposition. In Latin America, where Catholicism holds significant sway, the prevailing attitude is one where life is sacred from the moment of conception. This belief shapes stringent anti-abortion laws, as seen in countries like El Salvador and Honduras. Here, abortion is not merely a legal issue but a moral one tied deeply to the cultural and religious fabric. For many, terminating a pregnancy is viewed as contravening divine will, invoking strong ethical debates on personhood and the sanctity of life.

Africa presents a complex mosaic of attitudes towards abortion, influenced by a blend of indigenous beliefs, Christian missionary teachings, and Islamic principles. In countries like Nigeria and Uganda, abortion is heavily restricted, mirroring the moral and religious conservatism that permeates these societies. Yet, in South Africa, a more pragmatic approach prevails, with legal abortion services integrated into public health as part of broader reproductive rights. This highlights the continent's diverse cultural attitudes shaped by colonial history, religious teachings, and socio-political dynamics.

In Asian contexts, perspectives on abortion vary widely. In countries like China and India, where population control policies have historically dictated reproductive rights, abortion is often seen through pragmatic lenses linked to social and economic policies. In China, for instance, the one-child policy, though now relaxed, once made abortion a state-sanctioned necessity for controlling population growth. Meanwhile, in Japan, where there is both Buddhist influence and Western cultural integration, abortion is legal but less socially stigmatized, seen as a practical solution to social issues such as economic stability and family planning.

The Middle East, with its rich tapestry of cultures and religions, often reflects some of the strongest opposition to abortion. Islamic teachings, which emphasize the sanctity of life, play a crucial role in shaping laws and societal norms. However, there are nuanced interpretations within Islamic jurisprudence that allow for abortion under specific circumstances, such as to save the life of the mother. This demonstrates a complex balance between religious doctrine and practical health considerations that inform cultural attitudes toward abortion.

Throughout history, indigenous cultures have also held distinct perspectives on abortion, often tied to spiritual beliefs and communal practices. In many Native American tribes, for instance, traditional practices and shamanistic beliefs offer a unique spiritual context. These cultures might view abortion through a lens of spiritual balance, collective responsibility, and respect for ancestors and future generations, though modern influences have in many cases altered these views.

Despite these cultural differences, a common thread in the global narrative is the tension between tradition and modernity. Many societies experience a cultural clash between established values and the emergent global discourse on human rights and personal freedoms. This tension often manifests in legal battles, social movements, and contentious public debates, reflecting the ongoing struggle to reconcile cultural heritage with contemporary views on reproductive rights.

The discussion also spans significant ethical and moral dimensions, where questions about the beginning of life, moral responsibility, and individual rights transcend cultural boundaries. Philosophers, theologians, and ethicists from various traditions contribute to a dialogue that resonates globally, challenging societies to examine their beliefs and adapt to new understandings while honoring their cultural heritage.

In essence, cross-cultural attitudes towards abortion are a reflection of broader societal priorities, values, and belief systems. They demand a careful balancing act—one that reconciles individual rights and freedoms with collective moral and ethical responsibilities. As we consider these perspectives, we're reminded of the intricate and often personal implications of abortion within each cultural framework, underscoring the need for thoughtful dialogue and inclusive conversations that respect diversity while striving for a shared understanding of humanity's most profound issues.

Chapter 15: Alternatives to Abortion

In a world where despair often pushes mothers towards what they see as their only choice, discovering compassionate alternatives can feel like a light breaking through a dense fog. Adoption, while sometimes overshadowed by controversy, stands as a life-giving option that not only honors the sanctity of life but also enriches the family units longing to nurture those lives. Support systems, too, offer a crucial lifeline— networks of care that echo ancient communal values, ensuring that no woman walks this path alone. By surrounding expectant mothers with both emotional and practical assistance, society can transform adversity into hope, building a future where the dignity of every life, both mother and child, is revered and cherished. In embracing alternatives, we not only reject the hollow promises of an industry but also affirm a commitment to truth, love, and the timeless bonds of family.

Adoption as a Viable Option

Throughout human history, adoption has woven itself as a tapestry of love and sacrifice. It presents itself not just as a mere alternative to abortion but as a profound gesture that echoes through personal transformation and societal enrichment. Certainly, for many expectant mothers, the notion of navigating the turbulent waters of unplanned pregnancy brings fear and uncertainty. Yet within this challenging moment, adoption offers a beacon of hope and a testament to the enduring capacity for human kindness and selflessness.

One can't merely reduce adoption to a transaction of child rearing; it is fundamentally about giving life—a chance to nurture, grow, and flourish. It embodies a decision steeped in courage, one that prioritizes the child, offering them an opportunity to be loved and supported, while simultaneously providing a family with the gift of parenthood, which they might not otherwise experience. Adoption transcends the mere act of surrender—it becomes a life-affirming choice, tethered in the deep moral and ethical roots of civilization.

The value of adoption in the context of the abortion debate is not exclusively moral or ethical—it is also pragmatic. With adequate societal support, adoption becomes not merely an option but a viable and appealing choice. By fostering environments that support expectant mothers through crucial resources such as counseling, financial assistance, and housing, society can alleviate the burdens that often lead women to consider abortion.

Moreover, the ripple effects of embracing adoption resonate through society in profound ways. Beyond providing children with homes, it strengthens the social fabric, imbuing society with a spirit of acceptance and inclusivity. Every time a child is placed in loving arms, we're reminded of our shared humanity and interconnected destinies. Such acts spur communities toward greater empathy and solidarity.

It's essential to look at the role of the Church and religious organizations in promoting adoption. These institutions often serve as critical allies to both birth mothers and adoptive families, offering them not only material support but spiritual and emotional guidance as well. Through adoption, these organizations live out their mission of serving the vulnerable and protecting the sanctity of life.

On the other hand, adoption remains fraught with challenges and misconceptions. Some fear that placing a child for adoption means a lifetime of regret or uncertainty about their child's future. However, the increasing prevalence of open adoption, which allows for varying degrees of contact between birth parents and adoptive families, can help alleviate these concerns. Open adoption creates a space where birth parents can see their child grow up, maintain relationships, and be assured of their well-being.

Still, the adoption system itself requires improvement to ensure it is accessible, efficient, and fair. Legislative reforms and policy enhancements can help streamline the adoption process, making it less cumbersome and more navigable for all involved. Simplifying this system and reducing unnecessary bureaucratic barriers can encourage more families to consider adoption, thereby expanding its reach and impact.

Furthermore, public education campaigns can play a vital role in reshaping perceptions of adoption. By highlighting stories of successful adoptions and providing clear, accurate information about the process, misconceptions can be dispelled. Effective communication strategies can help underscore adoption's potential to transform lives positively, thereby encouraging more expectant mothers to view it as a feasible and honorable option.

Adoption, at its core, champions the dignity of life. It acknowledges and honors the inherent value of every human being, and in doing so, it aligns deeply with the Roman Catholic perspective that upholds life as sacred. Embracing adoption means recognizing and lifting up the lives entwined in this intricate dance—of birth mothers, adoptive parents, and above all, the children whose futures hang in the balance.

Ultimately, to perceive adoption as merely an alternative to abortion is to underestimate its transformative power. Adoption is an act of hope that echoes far beyond personal choice, resonating across generations. It represents life's triumph over despair, showcasing humanity's capacity to love and nurture beyond bounded circumstances.

As society navigates the multifaceted dynamics of reproductive choices, it is vital to advocate for policies and systems that truly support adoption as a viable option, fostering environments where every child can thrive. Compassionate advocacy, comprehensive support systems, and an unwavering commitment to life can together elevate adoption to its rightful place within the fabric of our communities.

Support for Expectant Mothers

In a world where alternatives seem limited and choices burdened with complexity, support for expectant mothers emerges as a beacon of hope. This section seeks to illuminate the multifaceted layers of assistance available to women who, facing bewildering circumstances, choose life over abortion. This decision, often shrouded in fear and uncertainty, deserves to be met with compassion, practical help, and unwavering support from society. The wonder and potential of bringing new life into the world can become more tangible with a network of support that reassures and uplifts.

For starters, it's crucial to understand that support can take many forms—ranging from emotional and material to medical and spiritual. Emotional support, often underestimated, forms the foundation on which all other types of assistance are constructed. Expectant mothers need compassionate counseling and mentorship, offering a listening ear and shared experiences that dissolve the isolation that too often accompanies unexpected pregnancies. Church communities have traditionally been pillars of emotional support, promoting the sanctity of life while extending a grace-filled hand to those in need.

Material support, on the other hand, bridges the gap between intention and action. Shelter, clothing, and nutrition are basic needs that can burden someone who's already grappling with the decision to embrace motherhood unexpectedly. Organizations dedicated to assisting these mothers provide not only the essentials but also empower them with resources such as job training and education, ensuring they can sustain themselves and their children in the long term. These practical measures work in tandem with the ethical and moral frameworks that invite mothers to view their pregnancies as a continuation of life's grand narrative rather than a detour.

Medical support is another indispensable pillar. Comprehensive healthcare for both the mother and the unborn child ensures that pregnancy progresses in the safest possible manner. Access to prenatal care and safe delivery options is paramount. It's through these medical avenues that potential complications are managed, nurturing not only the physical health of the mother and child but also easing mental burdens through the reassurance of expert care. In this respect, collaboration between healthcare providers and community support organizations amplifies the reach and efficacy of available services.

Yet, beyond these concrete forms of assistance lies the necessity for spiritual support. For expectant mothers who find solace within faith, spiritual guidance can offer profound comfort and direction. The Catholic Church, with its rich tradition, provides such refuge and guidance, emphasizing the profound dignity inherent in every human life. Through faith-based initiatives, expectant mothers discover a spiritual kinship that aligns them with a purpose larger than themselves, which can fortify them against societal pressures that trivialize or demean their choice for life.

It's important to recognize the societal structures that can enhance or hinder these support systems. Governments, local authorities, and nonprofit organizations each have roles to play in crafting policies and providing funding that make such support widely accessible and adequately funded. A collaborative approach that includes public and private entities can establish systematic networks offering sustained assistance to those navigating the rigors of unexpected pregnancy. Advocacy for these support systems must be steadfast, emphasizing that such investments bear not only individual but communal benefits that strengthen the moral fabric of society.

In order to maximize the effectiveness of such support systems, education plays a crucial role. Educating the public on the availability and importance of support networks shifts the narrative from a crisis-driven approach to one of hope and resilience. When widely understood and practiced, this educational endeavor embodies a structure where life is not only sustained but cherished, celebrated, and nurtured. Grassroots movements, driven ardently by both individuals and communities, aid this educational mission by personalizing the message and galvanizing local action.

In essence, support for expectant mothers cannot merely be an afterthought or an ancillary part of societal functions. It must be woven into the fabric of our communal life, a testament to our dedication to nurturing life at every stage. This support requires the cooperation of citizens, church, and state, each working to ensure that mothers facing unplanned pregnancies find themselves wrapped in a community that honors life through action, not just rhetoric. We owe it to them—to extend the promise of life in a way that is tangible, enduring, and transformative.

The journey of motherhood, especially when unexpected, need not be traversed alone. Let the love and support of a resolute community illuminate the path, dispelling the shadows of fear and uncertainty with the light of hope and solidarity. This vision emboldens us, taking us closer to a society where every mother feels empowered to choose life, knowing that the choice is championed by a multi-tiered support system that roots its wisdom in compassion, practicality, and unwavering faith.

Chapter 16: Legal Battles and Future Legislation

As we stand at the crossroads of history, the legal landscape surrounding abortion continues to be fiercely contested and profoundly consequential. Past court cases have set precedents that shape the present, yet they're merely the starting chapters of a more complex narrative that unfolds before us. The interplay between judicial decisions and burgeoning societal shifts suggests that abortion law is on the cusp of transformation. This is a battle not just for legal minds but for the soul of society, reflecting moral convictions and aspirations for the future. Like a tapestry woven with strands of hope and justice, future legislation will be crucial in balancing individual rights with the moral fabric of our communities. As lawmakers grapple with these issues, the potential implications on families, cultures, and the sanctity of life remain breathtakingly vast, demanding a comprehensive dialogue where ethics, compassion, and righteousness converge to guide the path ahead.

Key Court Cases and Decisions

In the vast tapestry of legal history, few issues have sparked as much societal debate as abortion. Over the decades, key court cases have not only shaped the legality of abortion but have also played a pivotal role in molding public perception and the socio-political landscape. From foundational rulings to recent decisions echoing across courtrooms, the stories behind these landmark cases reveal a complex interplay of law, morality, and humanity.

Perhaps the most foundational case is *Roe v. Wade* (1973). The Supreme Court's ruling established a woman's legal right to choose, effectively nullifying state laws that prohibited abortions. This decision, crafted amidst the socio-political upheaval of the 1970s, didn't just grant a legal right; it ignited a long-lasting national conflict between pro-life and pro-choice advocates. Roe's legacy lies in its creation of a constitutional framework that categorized abortion as a right under the umbrella of privacy. Yet, this landmark decision also sowed seeds of discord, with its implications reverberating through church pews and legislative halls to this day.

Following Roe, a series of cases emerged challenging and refining its precedents. A significant post-Roe ruling came with *Planned Parenthood v. Casey* (1992). This case reshaped the legal landscape by upholding the essence of Roe while allowing states to impose restrictions as long as they didn't place an "undue burden" on women seeking abortions. The decision subtly shifted the balance from a woman's autonomy towards a state's interest in potential life. This ruling exemplified the judiciary's struggle to balance individual liberties with societal ethical considerations.

Another pivotal case is *Gonzales v. Carhart* (2007), which addressed the permissibility of the Partial-Birth Abortion Ban Act of 2003. Unlike previous, more sweeping regulations, this ruling specifically targeted a particular abortion procedure. Upholding the ban, the Court highlighted a prevalent governmental stance prioritizing fetal life over the rights of women in certain contexts. Critics argue that Gonzales marked a notable regression in abortion access, reflecting a judiciary increasingly willing to accommodate state interests.

The legal battles surrounding abortion have consistently intersected with broader cultural dialogues, notably in *Whole Woman's Health v. Hellerstedt* (2016). This case scrutinized Texas legislation imposing strict requirements on abortion providers, posing a threat to the operational viability of clinics. The Court struck down these provisions, emphasizing the need for balancing regulatory intentions with actual health benefits for women. The decision reaffirmed the undue burden standard established in Casey, accentuating the judiciary's role as a guardian against excessive legislative encroachments.

More recently, *June Medical Services LLC v. Russo* (2020) demonstrated the ongoing tension over abortion rights. Similar to Hellerstedt, it evaluated a Louisiana law imposing admitting privileges on physicians. The decision underscored a fractured Supreme Court, narrowly maintaining the precedent while signaling potential shifts in judicial perspectives with changing court compositions. These rulings reveal a legal and moral battlefield, where the lines between regulation and infringement remain contentious and fluid.

In examining these court cases, one can't ignore the role of judicial philosophy and interpretation. Legal texts serve as battlegrounds for ideological slugfests, where constitutional meaning is woven into the fabric of societal norms. Each decision is more than just a legal outcome; it's a reflection of the cultural ethos of its time. Judges face the colossal task of interpreting laws that affect the corporeal and spiritual dimensions of life and death issues.

Moreover, the Catholic Church and numerous religious entities have tirelessly voiced their concerns, challenging the moral underpinnings of these rulings. They argue fervently for the recognition of the sanctity of life, from conception to natural death. Echoes of these struggles resonate in papal encyclicals, sermons, and grassroots movements, creating a moral counterpoint to judicial decrees.

The ripple effects of these decisions extend beyond courtrooms and legislative bodies. Lives are affected, tears are shed, and communities are galvanized into advocacy or protest. For pregnant mothers, each judgement represents not just a legal abstraction, but a personal reality with profound ethical implications. It reminds us of the stark dichotomy between a culture of life and one that embraces choice at such a contested human stage.

As society marches forward, the specter of future litigation looms large. The history of court decisions signifies a constant tug-of-war, ensuring that the dialogue around abortion remains vivid and vibrant. The tapestry of legal battles paints a dystopian landscape for some, where legislative gains against the backdrop of moral decline threaten the very fabric of familial and societal structure.

In sum, the journey through these key court cases unveils a saga of human frailty, courage, and the perpetual quest for justice. It's a narrative where the law entwines with moral conscience, begging for discernment and compassion. In the shadows of these rulings, the battle lines remain drawn, and the future of abortion rights hangs delicately in the balance.

The Future of Abortion Law

As society stands at the crossroads of history, the future of abortion law is poised for transformative change. In a world where technology, ethics, and morality intertwine, the debates surrounding abortion legislation invite both contemplation and action. The stakes are high, affecting women, families, and entire communities. To understand the future of abortion law, we must first examine the currents propelling this issue to prominence and unravel the complex web of social, moral, and legal threads weaving through the discourse.

Emerging from past rulings and cultural shifts, the dialogue on abortion law is increasingly shaped by technological advancements and ethical considerations. Innovations in medical science, such as improved imaging techniques and genetic testing, continue to redefine our understanding of fetal development. These advancements present lawmakers with new ethical dilemmas, challenging existing legal frameworks and demanding greater consideration of fetal rights versus reproductive freedoms. These scientific strides, while promising, also underscore the importance of clear, ethical guidance in legislative processes.

The potential for dystopian outcomes can't be ignored. Imagine a society where the sanctity of life is overshadowed by convenience and materialism, where unborn fetuses are commodified, mere subjects of choice, rather than beings with inherent dignity. Such a slippery slope demands vigilance. Lawmakers must weigh not just the immediate impact of legislation but its long-term implications on human values and societal norms.

At the heart of the abortion debate lies the moral vision of society. Some envision a world where policies reflect compassion, valuing both the mother and the unborn child. This perspective calls for laws that provide comprehensive support to expectant mothers, empowering them with real choices and resources to continue pregnancies if they so choose. It's a vision that aspires toward a society where life is cherished, and every child is deemed worthy of love and protection.

Drawing lessons from previous landmark court cases, the future of abortion law will likely involve a continued oscillation between state and federal authority. The enduring tension between states' rights and federal oversight hints at a legal landscape marked by variability and contention. While some states push for more restrictive laws that echo pro-life ideals, others may affirm more liberal stances, resulting in a patchwork of regulations that reflect the diverse moral fabric of the nation.

Further complicating the tapestry of future legislation are the economic and social undercurrents that drive policy decisions. The economic moguls of the abortion industry wield significant influence, shaping public opinion and, in some cases, swaying political agendas through lobbying efforts. The power dynamics at play demand transparency and accountability to ensure that laws serve the welfare of society rather than the interests of a few.

However, envisioning positive change in abortion legislation is not without hope. The future could herald a revival of ethical thinking that transcends partisanship. This shift would prioritize common humanity over division, illuminating a path where dialogue and understanding foster policies that respect the sanctity of life while acknowledging the complexities of individual circumstances. Such a future requires courage and empathy from lawmakers, public figures, and society at large.

Educational initiatives and advocacy efforts play a crucial role in shaping the future of abortion law. By raising awareness and informing young generations about the moral and ethical dimensions of abortion, there's potential to cultivate a culture of life, fostering respect and dignity for every human being. Education can transform hearts and minds, influencing legislation through an informed and morally grounded populace.

Ultimately, the future of abortion law will be decided at the intersection of ethics, technology, and cultural values. The journey is fraught with challenges, but it is also ripe with opportunities for profound societal healing and renewal. As new generations rise to take their place in the global conversation, the quest for justice and truth continues. With unwavering faith and unwavering love, let us nurture a future where laws reflect the deepest truths about human dignity, protection for the most vulnerable, and a commitment to the common good.

Chapter 17: Scientific Advancements and Their Impact

In an era where scientific advancements unfold rapidly, the unseen reverberations of these developments on the abortion debate are profound and multifaceted. Research on fetal development has illuminated the remarkable complexity of life in the womb, painting a picture that challenges the reductionist views often perpetuated by the abortion industry. As technology advances, we're ushered into a world where ultrasound imaging unveils the intricate dance of early life, lending a voice to the voiceless. Concurrently, future technologies, particularly those with ethical considerations, offer us a choice: a path leading towards compassion, empathy, and the preservation of life, or a descent into a dystopian disregard for the miracle of creation. This intersection of science and ethics raises pivotal questions about our collective moral compass and our innate responsibility to protect the sanctity of life, urging society to reassess the very foundation of its values.

Fetal Development Research

In the realm of understanding life's intricate tapestry, few things captivate as profoundly as the study of fetal development. It's a dance of divinely orchestrated complexity, where each stage unfolds with a unique beauty and purpose. As science peels back the layers of this process, it reveals a rich world within the womb—one that challenges us ethically, morally, and spiritually.

The journey of a fetus, from conception to birth, offers not only a scientific marvel but also an existential reflection. Recent advancements in technology have allowed researchers to delve deeper into the early stages of human life than ever before. Through detailed imaging techniques, such as 3D and 4D ultrasounds, we can observe the intricate development of organs, tissues, and even behaviors. Watching a heart develop and begin to beat at just 22 days post-conception inevitably evokes a sense of wonder.

These developments provoke questions beyond the data. They compel society to reconsider the moral imperatives regarding when life should be valued and protected. For instance, the growing body of evidence suggesting early fetal pain perception challenges prevailing thoughts in medical and ethical circles regarding pain and consciousness.

Consider, too, the dynamic evolution of a fetus's senses. Research has shown that by the second trimester, a fetus begins to respond to external stimuli—recognizing the mother's voice, reacting to music, and even showing signs of dreaming. Such findings don't merely bolster scientific curiosity; they challenge us to rethink the rhetoric surrounding fetal personhood and autonomy.

Advances in genetic research further illuminate this discourse. The mapping of the human genome has transformed our understanding of the genetic development that occurs in utero. This has implications not only for understanding congenital conditions but also for ethical conversations about potential genetic interventions. Here lies a tightrope between what is scientifically possible and what is ethically permissible.

In this context, the role of fetal development research becomes pivotal. These discoveries feed into larger societal debates, particularly impacting discussions about abortion. The more we know about fetal development, the harder it becomes to dismiss a fetus as merely a bundle of cells. The image painted by scientific research shows an ordered progression of life, defying simplistic narratives that deny the complexity of human development.

The intersection of faith and science here becomes crucial. Church teachings have long celebrated life from the moment of conception, viewing it as sacred and inviolable. These scientific findings echo a timeless truth—the inherent dignity of new life—from a secular angle. They complement spiritual truths with tangible evidence, fortifying the belief that life, at all stages, carries intrinsic value.

However, these research advances aren't devoid of controversy or misuse. There is a dystopian facet to consider when technology is wielded without ethical restraint. Practices like selective reduction or genetic manipulation risk transforming the womb into a battleground for ethical conflicts and societal control. Ensuring that these technologies serve life rather than commodifying it remains a pressing concern.

Thus, fetal development research embodies both the utopian vision of understanding and celebrating life's journey and the dystopian reality of its potential exploitation. It demands rigorous ethical scrutiny and a balanced approach that honors both scientific progress and unwavering moral foundations.

So, the tapestry of fetal development research extends beyond laboratories and academic journals. It weaves through cultural, moral, and spiritual dimensions—demanding of us a deeper introspection about our responsibilities to the unborn. As we stand at this juncture, it is not just a matter of cataloging stages of development but of understanding the profound implications they carry for the individual, family, and broader society. In learning about the wondrous journey from conception to birth, we inevitably learn more about ourselves and the society we shape.

Future Technologies and Ethics

As we gaze into the horizon of scientific advancement, the integration of technology within our daily lives becomes increasingly profound. Yet, we must question whether these advances genuinely uplift humanity or veer us toward a dystopian reality where moral considerations are overshadowed by technological prowess. In the realm of reproductive technologies, including those that pertain to abortion, it's crucial to weigh their implications thoroughly.

In modern times, innovations in genetics and embryology have opened a Pandora's box of possibilities that challenge our moral compass. One such area is fetal development research, which has uncovered astonishing insights into prenatal life. Indeed, the level of detail that scientists can now reveal about the developing fetus was once thought beyond reach. Still, with great knowledge comes great responsibility. There exists a pressing ethical quandary: how do we reconcile this scientific capability with our moral and spiritual beliefs?

The crux of the issue lies in the potential for technology to objectify human life. As prenatal imaging and genetic testing technology advance, they're often used not to celebrate life but to discern deviations from a subjective notion of "normalcy," leading to difficult ethical decisions. This burgeoning ability to closely examine and potentially manipulate human life in its earliest stages demands a rigorous ethical framework that respects the sanctity of life while acknowledging scientific advancements. We must ask ourselves: are we paving a path for compassionate care or a slippery slope toward eugenics?

Moreover, technologies like CRISPR and other gene-editing tools add another layer of complexity. These advancements allow for the alteration of genetic material, which might one day enable the modification of embryos to prevent diseases. While this seems utopian in its promise, it borders dangerously on playing God, raising ethical questions inherent in altering human lineage. What does it mean for our humanity if we begin to engineer life according to our desires? This debate isn't merely academic; it has tangible consequences on how society defines and values life.

Add to this the growing capability to sustain life outside the womb through artificial womb technologies, which might redefine viability and further complicate the discourse on abortion. Such advancements hold the promise of reducing maternal and fetal mortality but also pose existential and ethical questions. If technology offers alternatives to traditional gestation, what parameters of parental rights, responsibilities, and social constructs shift? The Roman Catholic perspective, steeped in reverence for life from conception, urges caution and deep reflection.

These future technologies intersect with ethical discourse on a global scale. On one end, advances could support the sanctity of life, providing alternatives that respect the unborn. Yet, they also risk dehumanizing fetuses, reducing them to scientific subjects whose worth is determined solely by their genetic makeup. It's a dual narrative teetering on the brink of either championing human dignity or diminishing it under the guise of progress.

As we venture into these uncharted technological territories, history provides its wisdom. Saints and scholars alike have emphasized that scientific endeavor should not divest us from our moral and ethical moorings. Much like St. Thomas Aquinas, who harmonized faith with reason, our contemporary challenge is to harmonize technological progress with unyielding ethical principles. It's in this harmonious balance that true advancement lies—not merely in innovation itself, but in innovation married to moral integrity.

The moral dilemmas presented by these advancements demand robust dialogue across all societal sectors. It involves examining the power dynamics at play in the tech industry, which often drives these innovations. As corporations invest in biotechnology and influence public policy, questions arise on their commitment to ethical practices. Conscious vigilance is needed to ensure decisions are guided by prudence rather than profit.

Ultimately, this journey into the future isn't isolated in the halls of academia or research facilities. It is a societal enterprise, one where pregnant mothers, ethical historians, and spiritual leaders must engage collaboratively. We need narratives that prioritize the inherent dignity of human life amidst these scientific marvels. The Roman Catholic viewpoint —with its emphasis on valuing life and fostering stewardship over creation—offers a critical lens to assess these advancements compassionately.

Given these considerations, we stand at a crossroads, where each step demands a choice. Do we adhere to a dystopian vision where ethics are constantly redefined to fit technological capabilities, or do we nurture a society that treasures humanity above innovation? In raising these questions and seeking answers grounded in moral conviction, we don't just forecast a future of ethical technology—we begin building it now.

Chapter 18: Advocacy and Education

In the realm of advocacy and education, it becomes imperative to illuminate and unravel the truth about abortion, forging a path toward understanding and compassion. Effective awareness campaigns are the beacon guiding society, dispelling the shadows cast by misinformation and misconception. In crafting these campaigns, it's crucial to utilize both the heart and the mind, employing narratives that resonate on a deeply human level while grounded in factual integrity. Meanwhile, educational strategies tailored for the youth must sow seeds of critical thinking, encouraging a forward-looking perspective that cherishes life and respects the sacredness of human dignity. History and theology entwine to provide a robust framework, underscoring the intrinsic value of every individual and the devastating societal ramifications when this value is compromised. By fostering a well-informed community, equipped with knowledge and empathy, we edge closer to a utopian vision—a society where abortion's harms are universally recognized, and life's sanctity is upheld and celebrated.

Effective Awareness Campaigns

In the ongoing battle for the sanctity of life, effective awareness campaigns stand as gauntlets, illuminating the truth amidst a web of deception spun by the abortion industry. They must not only educate but also resonate with the deepest corners of the human heart. It's no small task to disassemble the narrative that's been constructed by decades of skewed perspectives and misinformation. When crafted with care and conviction, these campaigns can pierce through the noise, awakening a dormant consciousness within society about the true cost of abortion. They operate at the intersection of knowledge, empathy, and moral clarity, each campaign needing to tailor its message to diverse audiences—from Roman Catholics and historians to the expectant mothers contemplating their choices.

The heart of any successful awareness campaign is its ability to connect narrative with witnessing—the act of sharing real stories that reflect the multifaceted impact of abortion on individuals and families. These stories breathe life into the statistics, offering faces and names to what otherwise might be abstract data. Testimonies from women and families who have endured the emotional, physical, and spiritual ramifications of abortion can serve as powerful catalysts for change. Each story acts as a beacon, reminding audiences of the profound human element at the center of this issue.

Visual storytelling plays a pivotal role in this endeavor. Engaging videos and images, like poignant portraits that capture the raw emotion etched in a mother's face or the hope residing in the eyes of a child who was adopted instead of aborted, can leave lasting impressions. Such media should be carefully crafted to portray both the loving potential of life and the tragic void left in its absence. It's the art of juxtaposing reality and possibility—showing what is against what could be—thereby mobilizing a call to action that lingers in the viewer's mind long after the campaign is over.

Strategic dissemination is also crucial. The message must reach into the digital corners where today's dialogues take place. Social media platforms, websites, and podcasts provide fertile ground for spreading awareness rapidly and effectively. By leveraging algorithms and strategic partnerships with influencers and trusted voices within communities, campaigns can achieve a reach that penetrates demographic and cultural barriers. This is an opportunity to blend ancient truths with modern technology, while maintaining a clear moral compass throughout the process.

Historically, the most effective campaigns are those that incorporate elements of utopian ideals—painting a vision of a society where life is revered and cherished. This vision should not shy away from illustrating the dystopian reality that arises when life is devalued. By creating a stark contrast, awareness campaigns can evoke a sense of urgency and moral responsibility in their audience. The mission is to ensure that the society chooses the path of light over darkness, life over death. It's about rekindling the inherent value of life in a way that does not merely appeal to the intellect but also resonates deeply with the heart and soul.

Moreover, these campaigns must exhibit unwavering courage in speaking out against the silent complicity that allows the abortion industry to continue its harmful practices unchecked. It's about breaking the silence, confronting apathy, and inspiring a collective moment of reflection. Campaigns can use historical and religious references, subtly threading these notions with the wisdom of figures like Saint Thomas Aquinas and GK Chesterton, to fortify their message with timeless principles.

An often-overlooked part of effective awareness is providing education alongside advocacy. This includes developing engaging curriculums and seminars that explore the truths and myths surrounding abortion, its implications on family and society, and the importance of alternatives like adoption. Empowering educators and religious leaders to disseminate this knowledge ensures that the roots of awareness grow deep, reaching youth before they are subjected to the half-truths they may encounter elsewhere.

This educational aspect can act as a supplementary layer, further grounding the ethical and moral foundations necessary for a societal shift.

It's about positioning the issue of abortion within its broader context, outlining the interconnectedness of life, morality, and social well-being. Such an approach not only raises awareness but also fosters critical thinking, enabling individuals to make informed, conscientious decisions.

To truly be effective, awareness campaigns must also bear witness to compassion. They should embody the tenets of love and understanding, recognizing the difficult situations that lead individuals to contemplate abortion and offering viable, supportive alternatives. Campaigns can collaborate with support groups, crisis pregnancy centers, and faith-based organizations to provide practical resources and emotional support for pregnant mothers contemplating their options.

In conclusion, effective awareness campaigns require a multidimensional approach, one that intertwines narrative, visual storytelling, strategic dissemination, and education with compassion and support. They must be relentless in the pursuit of truth while remaining anchored in love. If executed with precision and heart, these campaigns can pave the way for a societal transformation—a world where every life is acknowledged, respected, and cherished.

Educational Strategies for Youth

The formation of young minds is crucial, as the future rests in their hands. To effectively advocate for a culture of life and truth, educational strategies tailored for youth must be conscientiously developed and deployed. Educating youth about the complexities surrounding abortion is not just an effort in conveying facts; it is an endeavor of the heart, designed to evoke understanding and empathy while fostering a respect for life that transcends mere information.

Beginning in the early years, education can blend the innocence of childhood with the seeds of moral and ethical reasoning. Storytelling serves as one of the oldest and most resonant educational tools in forging this connection. Through parables, historical anecdotes, and narratives of hope, children can begin to grasp the sacredness of life and the tragedy inherent in its loss through abortion. These lessons need not be overtly didactic but instead woven subtly into stories that children can relate to, allowing them to derive meaning organically.

Moving into adolescence, the strategy shifts to engage critical thinking and personal reflection. Teenagers are naturally inclined to question authority and norms, making it imperative that they be equipped with tools to independently assess the abortion debate's moral and ethical dimensions. Socratic dialogue, debate clubs, and case study analyses can encourage them to scrutinize different perspectives. Here, the emphasis should be on empowering youth to explore the inherent dignity of human life, rather than prescribing a monolithic view.

In high school and college settings, a more formalized approach can be embraced, integrating comprehensive curricula that explore the historical, social, and scientific aspects of abortion. Courses that cover human development and fetal biology can elucidate the miracle of life at every stage, countering narratives that dehumanize or ignore the fetus's unique potential. Similarly, students can study the historical shifts in societal attitudes towards abortion, along with the roles of different cultural, religious, and social influences. This multi-disciplinary approach fosters a nuanced understanding, capable of challenging pervasive myths.

Furthermore, youth engagement initiatives can play a vital role in advocacy. Empowering young people to become peer educators transforms them from passive recipients of information to active proponents of life-affirming values. By fostering environments where teens can share insights and engage in advocacy efforts, they naturally become leaders in their communities. This peer influence is invaluable, as youth are often more receptive to messages coming from peers rather than authoritative figures.

Incorporating digital platforms into educational strategies is another vital component, considering the predominantly digital nature of contemporary youth culture. Harnessing social media, digital storytelling, podcasts, and interactive apps helps to disseminate life-affirming messages effectively. Online platforms can provide resources, host forums for discussion, and present testimonials in compelling formats that resonate with young audiences.

However, while leveraging technology, it is essential to instill discernment among youth to critically evaluate information sourced online. Media literacy programs that specifically address bias and misinformation in digital narratives around abortion can be instrumental. By teaching young people to identify media bias and critically engage with content, we empower them to form informed opinions rather than relying on one-sided or misleading digital content.

Christian communities have an influential role to play in shaping these educational strategies. By embedding these lessons within the framework of faith, young Catholics in particular can find alignment between their religious beliefs and their understanding of the abortion issue. Church-based youth groups, retreats, and mission trips can integrate teachings that reinforce respect for life, love, and compassion while emphasizing the inherent worth of each person as a creation of God.

Ultimately, educational strategies for youth must unify various approaches—incorporating intellectual pursuits, moral teachings, and emotional connections. They must address the whole individual, inspiring a generation committed to defending life. In empowering youth with knowledge, compassion, and conviction, we prepare them not only to counter the devastating impacts of abortion but also to become architects of a society that cherishes and upholds the sanctity of all human life.

Chapter 19: The Dehumanization of Fetuses

In a society increasingly driven by the semantics of the powerful, the language surrounding abortion stands as a chilling testament to the dehumanization of fetuses. This deliberate shift in language obscures the reality that within the womb exists a nascent human life, deserving of dignity and protection. In the name of autonomy and choice, the fetus is often reduced to a mere cluster of cells, stripped of identity or inherent rights. This linguistic maneuvering not only diminishes the fetus but accentuates a broader, more troubling trend: the erosion of the sanctity of life. As fetal rights are reframed as political bargaining chips, we confront a dystopian future where the worth of a human life is debated rather than affirmed. How did we arrive at a point where scientific wonders of fetal development are overshadowed by rhetoric designed to sanitize harsh truths? A society that fails to recognize and protect its most vulnerable risks losing its moral compass, an unsettling thought for all who cherish the values of empathy and human dignity. In contemplating these realities, we are called to defend a vision of the world that upholds the greatest good and ensures every life is seen, valued, and nurtured.

The Language of Abortion

To understand the depths of the abortion debate, one must dissect the language wrapped around it. Words have the power to shape reality, to cloud or clarify perceptions. In the discourse surrounding abortion, language often becomes a tool of persuasion and, at times, manipulation. The words chosen in this arena can dehumanize or humanize, simplify or complicate, largely depending upon the underlying agenda. This is quite evident in terms often used by proponents and opponents alike.

The term "fetus" stands at the heart of the discussion. In medical terms, a fetus is simply a developmental stage of a human being, yet in the abortion debate, it takes on different shades of meaning. For some, it's a way to depersonalize what they consider to be a cluster of cells, not yet deserving of the term "baby." By choosing clinical terminology, the conversation shifts and abstracts, leading individuals away from the visceral reality of potential life. Such language can evoke a sense of technicality rather than humanity.

In stark contrast, the term "unborn child" brings images of humanity and potential. It evokes emotional and ethical weight, reminding us of the individuality and future the fetus possesses. This language carries with it more than an acknowledgment of biological facts; it carries an ethical assertion that rings especially true for those of faith. For Roman Catholics, this language aligns with the belief that life begins at conception, and thus the "unborn child" should be afforded the dignity and rights of any human being.

Another term often encountered is "termination of pregnancy." This euphemism serves to sanitize the procedure, focusing on the cessation of a condition rather than its implications for the developing human life. By couching abortion in such terms, the profound moral and spiritual considerations that accompany the decision become blurred. This linguistic approach facilitates a clinical detachment, distancing both practitioners and patients from the moral ramifications taught by religious doctrine.

Within this linguistic landscape, the word "choice" emerges as a cornerstone. It frames the discourse in terms of individual rights and freedoms, often overshadowing the moral question of the right to life. "Pro-choice" advocates utilize this language to emphasize autonomy, a concept highly prized in modern society. Yet, for historians and the faithful, this simplification ignores the complex interplay of rights, such as the right to life of the fetus, and moral responsibilities advocated by the church.

Moreover, "reproductive rights" often encapsulates the abortion discourse, shifting focus away from the moral debate to that of human rights and health services. By doing so, it places abortion in the realm of personal healthcare rather than a societal or moral issue. In this paradigm, abortion becomes a service rather than a deeply personal decision with ethical implications—a shift that profoundly influences public perception and policy.

Efforts to humanize or dehumanize are further reflected in imagery and metaphor within language. Terms like "clump of cells" reduce the fetus to mere biology, devoid of individuality or potential. On the other hand, speaking of the fetus as a member of the human family introduces ethical considerations that appeal to shared human values and religious convictions.

The dehumanization seen in the language of abortion is not without societal consequences. By reducing human life to sterile terms, we risk desensitizing society to the moral gravity of abortion. Language shapes thought, and when thought is stripped of depth, societal values undergo erosion. Roman Catholics, historians, and compassionate mothers alike are called to recognize this linguistic dehumanization and to restore dignity through words that reflect truth and compassion.

The implications extend beyond individuals to the fabric of society itself. When language strips the human experience of its dignity, it impacts how communities perceive life and death. The challenge lies in ensuring language uplifts rather than diminishes, invites reflection rather than shuts down dialogue. In this endeavor, words must be chosen with precision to honor the complexity of human life that is at the heart of Roman Catholic teaching.

Language isn't merely descriptive; it's performative. It not only reflects reality but also shapes it. In the realm of abortion, manipulating language is akin to wielding power—power that influences societal norms and individual beliefs. The reductionist language of abortion impacts how future generations understand both the practice and its ethical implications. For pregnant mothers seeking guidance, words can obscure or illuminate the profound nature of the choice they face.

Thus, the task ahead for those invested in a compassionate and truthful discourse is clear: to reclaim language not just for clarity, but for the dignity of all involved. Abortion is not merely a medical or personal issue; it's a societal and moral issue that demands words that convey its seriousness and prompt reflection. Only then can we hope to foster a conversation where humanity, ethics, and faith occupy their rightful places in dialogue.

The significance of this conversation is underscored by its ultimate impact on the family and society. When the discussion is reduced to sterile terminology, the profound impact on women, families, and communities is often overlooked. Language must be wielded to build bridges of understanding, empathy, and hope that can lead to a brighter future marked by respect for life in all its stages.

The restoration of profound language in the abortion debate might pave the way for a deeper encounter with truth. It invites us to embody a culture of life that recognizes the interconnectedness of human experience and the sacredness of each life. For members of the Roman Catholic community, upholding this kind of discourse is not merely an intellectual pursuit but a moral imperative that honors the divine spark in each human being.

Understanding Fetal Rights

In the cacophony of debates surrounding abortion, the rights of the unborn often find themselves lost in the fray, overshadowed by the immediate concerns of socio-political agendas and individual freedoms. Yet, if we ought to assess our society's moral compass, it begins with how we view those who cannot advocate for themselves. Exploring fetal rights is not just an intellectual exercise; it is a profound moral inquiry that lies at the heart of dehumanization issues concerning fetuses.

The notion of fetal rights isn't a novel idea, nor is it confined to the boundaries of religious belief. Ancient civilizations wrestled with the value of unborn life long before modern legal systems were conceived. For many, these rights echo ancient principles of natural law, which inherently recognizes the dignity and worth of every human life from its inception. In fact, understanding fetal rights requires us to delve into a philosophical terrain where ontology meets ethics, forcing us to confront the very essence of what it means to be human.

Throughout history, various cultures, including the Roman Catholics, have articulated a singular truth: life begins at conception. This understanding isn't merely theological but is underscored by scientific advances that highlight distinct, vital human life even in the earliest stages. With the awe-inspiring complexity of fetal development, from the moment a sperm unites with an egg, a unique DNA sequence begins dictating the growth of a new human being. This intrinsic identity, unencumbered by social and legal statuses, demands recognition and respect.

However, as society grapples with this reality, the conversation becomes muddied with complexities. On one hand, modern legal frameworks often prioritize maternal rights, sometimes indirectly reducing the fetus to a mere cluster of cells with potential, not actual, personhood. On the other hand, the profound philosophical implications of granting fetal rights challenges the very fabric of personal autonomy as currently construed in many democratic societies.

Ironically, the dehumanization of fetuses—the systematic stripping away of their inherent rights—is bolstered by language. Euphemisms such as "terminating a pregnancy" or even more coldly "removing the pregnancy tissue" are employed to distance and desensitize individuals from the stark reality that what is being terminated is a growing, developing human life. Words carry power; when stripped of their humanizing elements, they marginalize the fetus from its rightful place in the moral universe.

Attempts to dismiss fetal rights often mirror dystopian elements reminiscent of fictional societies where certain groups are deemed less than human. Such narratives pave the way for moral blindness, allowing acts that society might otherwise find abhorrent. This sanitized lexicon serves as a tool of systemic dehumanization, shadowing potential moral atrocities in bureaucratic language. Recognizing these linguistic traps is paramount for historians and contemporary observers alike, lest we repeat the moral mistakes of the past.

For Roman Catholics, the denial of fetal rights not only contradicts spiritual teachings but erodes the societal acknowledgment of the sanctity of life—a cornerstone of their faith. Catholic doctrine espouses that every human life, from conception to natural death, bears the divine image and must be shielded under the aegis of justice and dignity. It's about invoking an ethical and spiritual awakening that transcends the transient changes in political ideologies or cultural fads.

Yet, convincing broader society hinges not only on religious or historical frameworks but also on addressing the philosophical and ethical implications holistically. Could recognizing fetal rights lead to a more compassionate, empathetic society that respects life at all stages? Public discourse often overlooks this perspective, so prevalent is the focus on tension between competing rights. Envisioning a world where both mother and child are simultaneously revered and cared for is the utopian challenge we must grapple with.

For the pregnant mother, understanding fetal rights can transform her experience. It's not merely a legalistic obligation but potentially an avenue for deeper connection with the burgeoning life within. Acknowledging these rights might inspire nurturing behaviors and attitudes, fostering healthier familial bonds long before birth. Encouraging pregnant mothers to appreciate the intrinsic value of their unborn children aligns with the ethos of honoring every individual's existential significance.

Beyond the individual, fostering an understanding of fetal rights invites society to assess its larger moral imperatives. The devaluation of fetal life becomes a precursor to broader societal desensitization. If the most defenseless among us can be disregarded, it sets a precedent for neglecting any vulnerable group. This underscores the importance of establishing a culture that respects, protects, and nurtures life at every stage.

In advocating for fetal rights, we are called to look beyond the constraints of politics and personal gain, to a vision more in line with the harmonious balance of moral integrity and social justice. This landscape invites scholars, theologians, and everyday citizens to participate in a redefined dialogue on human dignity. Such awareness can lead to policy changes, but more importantly, it may restore a shared commitment to life's inviolability—rekindling values that uphold our deepest humanitarian principles.

The struggle to recognize and uphold fetal rights is far from over. Yet, like a beacon amidst the storm, this discourse sheds light on the path toward greater compassion and unity. To foster an enduring legacy of life-affirming values, society must engage in earnest dialogue, transcending divisive rhetoric to embrace a vision of a world where every life is cherished, honored, and protected. It's both a profound responsibility and a noble pursuit worth the endeavor. As we move forward, let our actions prove the worthiness of every life, seen and unseen, in the tapestry that is our shared humanity.

Chapter 20: The Economic Influence of the Abortion Industry

The abortion industry's economic influence casts a shadow far-reaching and complex, entwining itself with political power and societal norms. Like a leviathan hidden beneath the surface, it drives an economic engine that, while lucrative, stands on moral quicksand. Clinics and corporations, fueled by substantial financial gains, exert an outsized influence through lobbying efforts and subtle corporate strategies. This influence infiltrates political corridors, shaping legislation and public policy that often contradicts the ethical foundations valued by many communities. With every transaction, an unsettling alliance forms between economic incentives and the devaluation of life, creating an economy where the sacred is commodified. This dystopian reality challenges us to ponder the true cost of prosperity birthed from such an enterprise, which, while profiting a few, erodes the moral and societal fabric for many.

Financial Power of Clinics and Corporations

The economic influence of abortion clinics and corporations stands as a towering testament to their financial might, shaping healthcare landscapes and wielding significant influence over societal norms. At the heart of this system lies an expansive network of clinics profiting from a service beset with ethical debates, yet undeniably lucrative. Clinics don't simply operate as isolated entities; they are often extensions of larger corporations whose reach extends far beyond the local community. These corporations know the market, supply the demand, and in doing so, accumulate vast sums of wealth. It's a tightly woven tapestry where money and morality clash, and the financial interests of some can overshadow the lives of many.

Clinical operations within the abortion industry reflect a business model that prioritizes volume and efficiency. Clinics are often located in areas with high-demand potential, strategically placed to maximize client flow. The geographical concentration isn't by accident; rather, it's a calculated decision made by the corporations that own or fund many of these clinics. Such decisions highlight the corporate world's knack for capitalizing on demands, creating a cycle that feeds financial power and sustains the industry's grip on a delicate facet of healthcare. While clinics provide a service, the overarching corporations thrive on profitability, ensuring that the wheels of this industrial complex continue to turn smoothly.

It's important to consider the scale of operations when reflecting upon the economic might of these clinics and corporations. Some function under nonprofit status yet manage budgets comparable to major corporate players. The veneer of humanitarian service can mask the underlying profit-driven motives. Behind the charitable facade lies a sophisticated business model bolstered by substantial revenues, enabling continued expansion and entrenchment in the medical field. The profits generated by these clinics not only sustain current operations but also fuel future growth and lobbying efforts.

Indeed, the reach of abortion corporations stretches into political spheres, with wealth granting them a voice in policy-making that echoes far and wide. Through lobbying, they seek to influence legislation that could either bolster their presence or threaten their profits. Political contributions become investments in future earnings, making corporations formidable participants in policy debates. This financial fortification allows them to advocate for regulations—or lack thereof—that align with their economic interests, often at odds with public sentiment or ethical stances.

Underneath the layers of financial power, one finds a potent promotional machine striving to normalize and market their services under the guise of healthcare necessity. Corporate branding and strategic advertising campaigns are designed to mold public perception, cultivate acceptance, and encourage consumer trust. The language is carefully crafted, the imagery meticulously chosen, all aimed at solidifying the corporation's place as not just a service provider but a necessary component of modern medicine.

Yet, this financial power isn't isolated; it trickles down, affecting numerous aspects of life. Communities, for instance, can become economically reliant on clinics, viewing them as job providers and financial contributors through taxes and local business engagement. In many places, clinics are amongst the largest local employers, embedding themselves deeply within the community's economic structure. This economic symbiosis can even lead to a form of silence regarding ethical concerns, as dependency on the clinic's economic contributions outweighs moral debates.

Moreover, the economic sway of clinics and corporations influences healthcare practices and education. They fund research, sponsor educational initiatives, and even provide training for healthcare professionals. While contributing positively to medical knowledge, there's a risk of bias, as funded research often aligns with the corporate narrative. Educational content might skew towards promoting services provided by the companies themselves, perpetuating a cycle where financial incentives dictate knowledge dissemination.

The financial power of these entities also extends into technology, where investments in medical and digital advancements ensure they remain at the forefront of the healthcare field. Cutting-edge medical technologies offer clinics new methods to operate more efficiently and securely, while digital platforms expand their advertising reach and facilitate patient management systems. This technological leverage not only sustains their business model but enhances their profitability, proving essential in maintaining their dominant position in the industry.

Questions about the sustainability and ethical underpinnings of this financial structure proliferate, particularly as dissonance grows between profit motives and human dignity. Many argue that the prioritization of profit over ethics results in compromised care, where business interests override patient welfare. It's in this tension that the true cost of the abortion industry's financial clout becomes apparent, calling into question whether economic success justifies overshadowing broader healthcare goals and moral considerations.

Reflecting upon the financial power wielded by abortion clinics and corporations deepens the understanding of their pervasive impact on society. It challenges individuals to consider the real cost of such influence—not just in dollars and cents but in the ethical fabric of society. As these entities continue to amass resources and extend their reach, they shape the medical landscape while leaving in their wake a trail of moral and social questions that beg for thoughtful consideration.

Lobbying and Political Influence

The abortion industry wields significant power through its extensive lobbying efforts and political influence. This influence is not merely an incidental aspect of its operations but a core strategy to ensure its interests are protected and advanced at every level of government. Consider the magnitude of resources devoted to shaping policy decisions: financial capital flows vigorously towards campaign contributions, targeted lobbying efforts, and strategic alliances with political entities. These activities reflect a deliberate and concerted effort to embed the abortion industry within the fabric of legislative decision-making.

Lobbying, as a mechanism of influence, has long been wielded by various industries to promote favorable legislative and regulatory environments. The abortion lobby is no different, yet its methods and impacts are uniquely far-reaching, embedding themselves deep within societal structures. By financially backing sympathetic legislators and supporting political action committees (PACs), the industry aligns itself with powerful players to perpetuate its objectives. These alliances manifest in legislation that often leans towards increased access to abortion services, government funding, and protective regulations for clinics, buffering them against lawsuits and scrutiny.

It's critical to recognize the dualistic nature of pro-abortion lobbying. On one hand, there is the overt and often public-facing advocacy that seeks to champion reproductive rights under the banner of personal choice and freedom. This message is skillfully crafted to resonate with contemporary values of autonomy and equality. On the other hand, there's a subtler, perhaps more insidious, layer of influence that operates behind closed doors. It is here that lobbyists work tirelessly to influence lawmakers, leveraging data, reports, and strategic narratives designed to nudge policy in favor of the industry.

The scope of political influence extends beyond domestic borders as well. Internationally, organizations advocating for abortion rights collaborate with global entities to promote policy changes in countries with restrictive abortion laws. These efforts involve substantial lobbying at global institutions such as the United Nations, aiming to embed reproductive rights within international human rights frameworks. This transnational approach not only amplifies the industry's influence but also portrays its agenda as a universal moral imperative, thus normalizing the practice on a global scale.

Delving deeper, it's apparent that the abortion industry's political clout is not solely reliant on external entities. Significant portions of its financial resources are allocated to fostering advocacy from within, creating and supporting grassroots movements that champion its cause. These movements, often youth-focused, are bolstered by educational initiatives and campaigns that subtly shift public opinion and perceptions on abortion. Through educational curriculums, media campaigns, and influencer partnerships, the industry ensures its narrative remains relevant and pervasive.

Moreover, the relationship between the abortion industry and media narratives cannot be overlooked. By supporting media outlets and influencing journalistic content, the industry can frame public discourse to its advantage, aligning media representations with its strategic objectives. This connection between media influence and legislative backing forms a feedback loop that reinforces the industry's standing, ensuring that attempts to counter its influence are met with robust opposition and a well-honed narrative.

The ramifications of such pervasive lobbying are evident in the legislative landscape. Over the years, despite various challenges, there has been a steady relaxation of regulations surrounding abortion services in many jurisdictions. Legal battles, often portrayed as epic battles over fundamental rights, are frequently backed by the powerful presence of the lobby, ensuring that the industry's stance is well-represented and, more often than not, prevails in courtrooms across the nation.

However, this immense influence is not without its detractors and backlash. A growing awareness among communities, spurred by moral, ethical, and religious concerns, particularly within Catholic circles, has led to increased resistance. Many argue that the lobbying efforts fundamentally distort democratic processes, prioritizing industry profitability over human life and societal well-being. This pushback highlights a critical tension between financial interests and moral imperatives that continues to shape the abortion debate.

Ultimately, the lobbying and political influence exerted by the abortion industry invite profound questions about the nature of democracy, the sanctity of life, and the role of money in shaping public policy. These intertwined dilemmas challenge us to reflect deeply and act decisively. As such, the discourse surrounding the industry's lobbying practices is not just an examination of political tactics but a call to ethical and moral introspection.

Chapter 21: Addressing Misconceptions About Abortion

In the swirling discourse surrounding abortion, myths often shroud the reality, perpetuating confusion and misunderstanding. One misconception suggests that abortion is a simple medical procedure without long-term consequences. Yet, this narrative masks the profound psychological, physical, and societal impacts faced by women and families. Some contend the procedure empowers women, liberating them from unwanted pregnancies, but such claims often overlook the emotional scars and societal pressures that accompany these decisions. The notion that access to abortion unequivocally equates to women's rights fails to account for the myriad moral and ethical dilemmas intrinsic to the act. Unfounded beliefs about the absence of fetal pain or development diminish the human dignity at the heart of the issue. To truly address these misconceptions, one must approach this complex topic with an understanding rooted in empathy, scientific truth, and moral reflection. Dispelling these myths is paramount to unveiling the stark realities of abortion's influence on individuals and society, challenging us to embrace informed and compassionate dialogues.

Common Myths and Realities

In the swirling current of discourse surrounding abortion, myths often rise to the surface, clouding judgment and distracting from the truths beneath. These myths can shape opinions and, sometimes, even pivotal decisions. It is vital to sift through these misconceptions to reveal the reality that lies beneath.

A prevalent myth suggests that abortion is a straightforward medical procedure, devoid of lasting impacts. However, the reality is starkly different. Abortion can have serious psychological and physical implications, affecting not only the woman but also the family and broader society. For many, the journey doesn't end with the procedure. Emotional and mental health struggles frequently persist, requiring ongoing care and attention. The narrative that dismisses these potential consequences does a disservice to the individuals who face them.

An equally insidious myth posits that the abortion industry acts purely out of concern for women's health. In reality, the industry often operates with its own interests at the forefront, driven by financial gain and political power. Clinics and corporations wield significant influence, lobbying for legislation that aligns with their agendas rather than prioritizing the well-being of the women they purport to serve. This truth uncovers a troubling dynamic where women's bodies become battlegrounds for profit and political clout.

Religious perspectives are frequent targets of misconception. Some believe that all religious institutions unequivocally oppose abortion, presenting a black-and-white stance. Yet, the reality is more nuanced. While many religious doctrines value life from conception, interpretations and teachings can vary. Within the Roman Catholic Church, for instance, the sanctity of life is emphasized, but historical context and theological insights offer layers of understanding. It's crucial to acknowledge these complexities rather than reductively categorizing religious views as monolithic opposition.

Another enduring myth is the belief that those who are pro-life lack compassion for expectant mothers facing difficult decisions. The reality is quite the opposite. Pro-life movements often extend support networks for women, offering alternatives like adoption and providing resources for expectant mothers. The compassionate outreach intended to uphold both the mother's and the unborn child's dignity highlights an often-overlooked dimension of the debate.

Among the troubling myths is the notion that fetuses are nothing more than a collection of cells until birth. Advances in science and fetal development research reveal a more complex picture. By understanding the humanity and intricate development occurring within the womb, we challenge the narratives that reduce the fetus to mere biological matter. This comprehension underscores the ethical and moral dimensions in decisions about abortion, elevating the conversation from biological simplicity to human significance.

Yet another myth assumes that access to abortion universally empowers women, granting them complete freedom over their reproductive choices. However, many women feel coerced by societal pressures or economic circumstances, finding themselves in positions where abortion feels less like a choice and more like an obligation. True empowerment involves providing women with real options and support, not funneling them toward a single, often painful, decision.

Addressing these myths head-on is vital for fostering a more enlightened discussion around abortion. As we continue to peel away the layers of misconceptions, we enable clearer visibility into a subject mired in complexity and emotion. We owe it to ourselves and future generations to understand the full scope—emotional, ethical, and societal—of this deeply impactful issue.

In unmasking these realities, we're compelled to reflect on our values and the kind of society we wish to create. The myths surrounding abortion have been pervasive for far too long, influencing not just personal choices but also shaping the societal ethos. By grounding ourselves in truth and compassion, we can pave the way for a future that cherishes life and respects the dignity of all mothers and their unborn children.

Countering Misinformation

In today's world, where information flows freely and often unchecked, misinformation about abortion permeates not only public discourse but the deeply personal decisions of individuals. Understanding how to counter this misinformation is vital for safeguarding the truth and protecting the dignity of human life. This undertaking requires persistent effort to disentangle well-entrenched myths from the solid ground of reality. The abortion debate, as sprawling and complex as it is, cannot allow space for deceptions that misguide those it affects most directly: individuals contemplating abortion, families, and society at large.

The first step in combating misinformation is recognizing its various forms: deliberate falsehoods, half-truths, and omissions that distort perceptions. One common misconception is the belief that abortion is a safe and straightforward procedure, an idea propagated by its normalization in some channels of media and the tacit endorsements of influential figures. However, extensive research and countless personal stories reveal a multitude of complications, both physical and emotional. By addressing this disparity, we can begin to cultivate a more honest narrative.

To further illustrate, consider the widely circulated notion that abortion has no long-term effects on a woman's health. This assertion, often backed by selective data points, minimizes the significant physical and psychological repercussions documented in numerous studies. The mental health challenges, including depression, anxiety, and post-traumatic stress disorder, should not be dismissed as mere byproducts but rather given the weight they deserve in the conversation around abortion. Recognizing these truths helps us support women in healthier, more informed ways.

Our responsibility extends beyond acknowledging existing misinformation; it involves educating others and spreading awareness based on factual evidence and empathy. Education begins with debunking myths that have persisted over decades. This includes clarifying the misunderstanding that abortion primarily concerns individual autonomy without societal consequences. In reality, the ripple effects on communities and family structures are profound, influencing cultural dynamics and values. It is essential to appreciate the broader picture to counter simplistic narratives that ignore complex consequences.

The language used in discussions about abortion also plays a crucial role in perpetuating or countering misinformation. The semantic choices employed can dehumanize fetuses or oversimplify the gravity of the decision. Terms are powerful; they shape our consciousness and influence public perception. To counter misinformation effectively, we should strive for language that respects human life at every stage, underscoring its inherent dignity without resorting to euphemisms or sensationalism.

Another prevalent myth is that abortion is a necessary evil required to prevent greater societal despair, a notion championed as if there are no viable alternatives. Yet numerous case studies illustrate how adoption and comprehensive support systems for expectant mothers can provide compassionate solutions without compromising ethical principles. Highlighting these alternatives challenges the misinformation that often paints a dire, binary choice between abortion and untenable hardship.

The media's role in shaping public opinion on abortion cannot be overstated. By dissecting media bias, we gain tools to discern objective reporting from narratives that may lean towards advocacy in disguise. Analyzing case studies where media portrayal has influenced public sentiment illuminates the pathway towards responsible journalism, where accuracy reigns supreme. Promoting critical media literacy helps the public navigate the information they consume, fostering informed opinions rather than inherited biases.

Encouraging open dialogue rather than polarizing confrontation helps cultivate environments where misinformation can be corrected through shared understanding. Creating spaces for respectful discussions, where diverse perspectives are weighed thoughtfully, is crucial. Fostering respectful debates that emphasize empathy over dogma opens doors to correcting misinformation, replacing contention with constructive conversation.

In the quest to counter misinformation, we must engage with those affected by abortion with compassion and understanding, rather than condemnation. It is through authentic dialogue that bridges are built, facilitating truthful exchanges that transcend preconceived notions. As such, efforts to address misinformation should be underscored by sincerity and a genuine desire for collective enlightenment.

Countering misinformation about abortion is not merely an academic exercise; it is a moral imperative with profound ethical implications. The truth bears consequences that reach into the heart of our society, affecting families, communities, and the very fabric of our culture. By dedicating ourselves to truth, we concurrently champion the sanctity of life and the potential for a brighter future where every life is valued and protected.

Chapter 22: Support Systems for Post-Abortion Recovery

In the journey through the often tumultuous aftermath of abortion, a constellation of support systems emerges as vital lifelines for recovery. These systems, grounded in compassion and understanding, play a crucial role in the healing process, not only for the individuals directly involved but for families and communities touched by the ripple effects. Counseling services offer a professional sanctuary where a safe space for dialogue and reflection is fostered, allowing individuals to navigate the labyrinth of emotions that follow. Meanwhile, community and faith-based organizations, with their rich tapestry of spiritual and emotional support, provide a sense of belonging and hope. They become a haven for shared experiences and collective healing, echoing a path toward a society striving to uphold dignity and restoration. In a world that sometimes overlooks the deep scars left by abortion, these support networks become beacons of solace and strength, reminiscent of an ideal where every soul finds its peace—a true testament to the power of human empathy and aid.

Available Counseling Services

In the aftermath of an abortion, many women find themselves grappling with a spectrum of emotional and psychological challenges. These burdens are not just invisible; they can be profoundly isolating. However, it is in this intricate landscape of recovery where counseling services play an indispensable role. The presence of compassionate and knowledgeable counselors can offer a sanctuary—a safe space where individuals are free to express their deepest emotions and begin the journey of healing.

The effectiveness of counseling services hinges largely on their ability to be multifaceted, addressing the diverse needs of those seeking assistance. From individual therapy sessions to group discussions, each format offers unique benefits. Individual counseling focuses on personalized care, allowing women to delve into their experiences at their own pace. It becomes a mirror, reflecting their struggles and strengths, and guiding them through the labyrinthine feelings of loss, guilt, or even relief.

Group therapy, on the other hand, fosters a sense of community among those who might otherwise feel alienated. Sharing stories and hearing others speak their truths can be powerfully validating. It not only aids in diminishing the weight of solitude but also encourages collective healing—a reminder that one is not alone in their experience. For some, this can be a cornerstone of reclaiming their peace and moving forward with resilience.

Various organizations have understood the profound necessity for these services and have formed a network of support that spans both secular and faith-based approaches. Faith-based counseling, in particular, attempts to reconcile the emotional wounds of abortion with spiritual beliefs. This type of counseling provides a unique approach that melds psychological healing with spiritual growth, offering Roman Catholic women—and others—an avenue to explore forgiveness and renewal through their faith.

One cannot underestimate the power of faith-based counseling, as it often intertwines the rich tapestry of doctrine with the lived experiences of those recovering post-abortion. Embracing a Christian worldview, these programs respect the person's journey and dignity, allowing them to explore paths to atonement that resonate deeply with their core beliefs. Importantly, such counseling refrains from condemnation but instead emphasizes love, compassion, and restoration—a hallmark of the Catholic ethos.

Secular counseling services are equally crucial, focusing on evidence-based practices to help women navigate their emotions without necessarily invoking religious contexts. These services often utilize cognitive-behavioral techniques, mindfulness practices, and other therapeutic interventions that empower individuals to reshape their thoughts and behaviors. By promoting mental wellness within a non-religious framework, secular counseling broadens accessibility, ensuring that all women, irrespective of their beliefs, have the opportunity to heal in a way that suits them.

Moreover, the role of prenatal care centers and community outreach programs cannot be overlooked. Many of these organizations provide free or low-cost counseling services, making them available to women across various socioeconomic backgrounds. These centers aspire not just to heal but to educate, offering workshops and resources that inform women of their options both pre- and post-abortion. Education, in this sense, becomes a balm in itself—equipping women with knowledge that can prevent future trauma.

In a dystopian vision where abortion is stripped of its human context, where it is seen merely as a procedure devoid of emotional aftermath, counseling services rescue the narrative. They remind us that every statistical number represents a life touched, a story altered. These services endeavor to weave back the frayed edges of the human experience, acknowledging that true recovery encompasses the heart and soul as much as the mind.

There are also specialized services dedicated to addressing the unique needs of families affected by abortion. Often, the ripples of an abortion decision extend beyond the person who undergoes the procedure, embroiling partners, extended family, and even friendships in the emotional aftermath. Such services provide a platform for open dialogue and reconciliation, encouraging healthy communication and mutual understanding among loved ones.

Considering the historical context of abortion and counseling within the Catholic tradition, one might find it paradoxical that a Church with such a staunch stance on abortion could nurture a space for post-abortion healing. Yet, it is precisely within this rich historical and moral framework that Catholics find both the strength to uphold life and the compassion to support those who have experienced abortion. This duality is manifest in traditional rehabilitation programs, retreats, and spiritual guidance designed to envelop women in understanding while encouraging them towards transformative recovery.

Ultimately, available counseling services form the backbone of post-abortion recovery systems. They are the quiet but steadfast stewards of those seeking to mend, offering a return to wholeness and hope. It is an ongoing invitation to rebuild, one person at a time, with each story of survival adding a brushstroke to the canvas of shared human experience. These services are a testimony to the enduring belief that there is healing beyond hurt, and life beyond loss.

Thus, as we evaluate the broad spectrum of supportive measures available today, one salient truth emerges: counseling services are not just a remedy for post-abortion trauma, but an essential component of a society striving to affirm the inherent dignity and sanctity of the human person. In this light, they become not merely a safety net for those who have fallen but a bridge to a future shaped by empathy, grace, and a renewed commitment to life.

Community and Faith-Based Support

In the journey toward healing after an abortion, the role of community and faith-based support cannot be understated. These systems provide a sanctuary, a place where emotional, spiritual, and physical recovery can intersect in nurturing and transformative ways. For many, the road to recovery might appear daunting, littered with societal judgments and personal regrets. Yet, amidst this landscape, community and faith-based initiatives stand as beacons of hope, offering solace, kindness, and understanding—a true testament to humanity's capacity for empathy.

Communities, in their various forms, have always held the power to uplift individuals through collective strength. In the context of post-abortion recovery, this support takes on unique dimensions. Community groups provide a network where individuals can share experiences, address feelings of isolation, and engage in a common dialogue about their struggles and hopes. Whether through formal gatherings or informal meet-ups, these interactions foster a sense of belonging and validation, crucial elements that can aid in personal healing.

Faith-based organizations, drawing from centuries-old traditions of healing and reconciliation, create a spiritual dimension to the support network. These organizations ground their work in compassion, rooted in the teachings which emphasize forgiveness, mercy, and renewal. Engaged in this labor of love, clergy and laypeople alike offer counseling services that are both spiritually enriching and deeply personal. Here, individuals find a safe space to explore their emotions within the context of their faith, guiding them toward forgiveness and acceptance.

It is curious to consider how faith-based support systems draw on religious narratives to facilitate healing. The tales of transformation and redemption, so prevalent in sacred texts, act as a mirror reflecting the potential for renewal inherent in every individual. These narratives provide not just comfort, but a model for experiencing and surviving suffering, suggesting that pain, when embraced, can be a channel for profound personal growth. It is through these teachings that the faithful might find the fortitude to reconcile their past actions with their present selves.

Moreover, faith organizations often extend beyond spiritual guidance to offer practical support, addressing the diverse needs of those they serve. This might include access to medical care, financial aid, or shelter, recognizing that holistic healing encompasses both the body and the soul. By addressing these multifaceted needs, communities underscore their commitment to nurturing each person's dignity and self-worth.

In considering the breadth of support available, it is also worth acknowledging the role of specific programs designed to aid post-abortion recovery. Many churches and religious groups have developed targeted initiatives, such as retreats, workshops, and peer support meetings. These initiatives are carefully crafted to respect and honor the individual journeys of participants, providing them with the tools to navigate their emotions and rebuild their lives. The success of these programs often lies in their ability to foster authentic connections, allowing participants to feel seen and heard.

A remarkable aspect of community and faith-based support lies in its emphasis on forgiveness and reconciliation, not only with oneself but also with the wider community. Such reconciliation efforts aim to bridge the gap between personal convictions and community expectations, offering a path to restoring harmony within the broader social fabric. Forgiveness becomes not merely an interior act but a shared endeavor, one that reinforces communal bonds and aids the healing process.

Indeed, while the path of healing is intensely personal, it is through the intertwined support of community and faith-based systems that individuals can truly flourish. By engaging with these networks, those recovering from abortions are reminded that they are not alone, that their struggles and triumphs form part of a larger human experience. And in this larger tapestry, every story has value, every wound has the potential for healing.

As we reflect on these aspects, it is essential to acknowledge the compelling vision these support systems embody—a world where compassion reigns, where every person's journey is honored, and where healing is a shared mission. It is this hope that community and faith-based support strives to cultivate, offering a future brightened by the promise of renewal and the enduring power of love.

While not without their challenges, these support systems hold within them a profound ability to change lives, transforming despair into hope and alienation into community. As those who walk the path of post-abortion recovery find new life in these supportive environments, they also contribute to the ever-expanding circle of care and compassion that defines the human spirit.

Chapter 23: The Spiritual Consequences of Abortion

In a world where choices are often tangled in complexities, the spiritual ramifications of abortion remain a profound mystery, challenging the soul's very essence and harmony. While societal debates frequently revolve around physical and emotional aftermaths, the spiritual disquiet lingers, often unacknowledged. This wound cuts through the fabric of faith and morality, leaving scars that may not be visible but are deeply felt by those who grapple with it. The Church, with its age-old wisdom, offers solace and guidance, urging a return to spiritual authenticity and healing. It stands as a beacon, urging reconciliation with oneself and the Divine, advocating for a journey of redemption. In embracing the sanctity of life, one begins the profound process of healing, which calls for introspection, forgiveness, and a renewal in grace. This spiritual odyssey, though daunting, is an invitation to rediscover hope and restore a connection with the Creator, acknowledging that every soul is precious and deserving of love and peace.

Soul Searching and Healing

Abortion isn't just a medical procedure; it slices through the very fabric of spiritual and emotional well-being. This journey often ignites a deep inner conflict, pushing individuals into a realm of self-reflection and spiritual questioning. The soul, once at peace, now finds itself tangled in layers of doubt and sorrow, yearning for a sense of reconciliation and healing that can be elusive yet essential. This part of the journey is both personal and universal, demanding honest confrontation with one's beliefs and values.

The initial reaction to abortion might range from relief to profound grief, but often, as time stretches on, feelings of emptiness emerge. This void can lead to an existential crisis, compelling individuals to engage in soul searching—a quest not just for answers, but for meaning and purpose. It's a complex process, where the present self must come to terms with past decisions, and where future steps are influenced by the lessons learned.

This path towards healing involves grappling with questions that probe the essence of one's existence and moral framework. Many turn to their faith traditions for support, seeking solace in ritual and community. For Roman Catholics, this journey is often intertwined with penitence and the sacraments, providing a spiritual balm for wounded souls. The Church, with its rich tradition of forgiveness and redemption, offers a sacred space where individuals can seek reconciliation both with God and with their own inner selves.

Within the context of Roman Catholicism, the sacrament of Confession plays a significant role. It is here, in the quiet confines of the confessional, that one might pour out the burdened heart, seeking absolution and the grace to move forward. This sacred tradition acknowledges the weight of sin but, more importantly, emphasizes God's boundless mercy and love. It is a critical step for many in rebuilding their inner spiritual harmony.

Yet, healing is not instantaneous; it's a pilgrimage that extends over time, often with setbacks along the way. It's not uncommon for individuals to revisit feelings of guilt or shame, emotions that require continuous nurturing and guidance. This is where community support becomes invaluable. Engaging with others who have faced similar challenges can offer a profound sense of solidarity and understanding, reminding people they are not alone on this path.

Support groups, especially those grounded in faith, provide an environment where emotions can be openly shared and spiritual growth encouraged. These communities become a lighthouse, guiding the lost back to safe shores. Participants find shared strength and wisdom, learning from each other's experiences. The communal aspect of healing shines a light on how interconnected we are, how each of our journeys impacts others.

This transformative process of soul searching and healing also opens up avenues for personal growth that may not have been apparent before. Reflecting deeply on life choices often reveals new paths, new purposes, and a renewed vigor for life. It's about discovering what truly matters and aligning one's actions with deeply held values. This process, albeit painful, can become a catalyst for profound change.

Within this journey, there's a dawning realization that healing does not mean forgetting. Remembering is crucial—it strengthens resolve and teaches compassion, turning sorrow into a beacon of hope for others. For some, this might mean becoming advocates for life, using their stories to educate and inspire. For others, it means quiet reflection, finding peace within and extending that peace to the world around them.

Historically, the Church has recognized the depths of spiritual consequence and has always been a beacon of hope and renewal. The teachings on forgiveness are not merely lip service but foundational elements that have guided countless souls toward healing. In this regard, the Church dialogs openly about the spiritual consequences of abortion and the pathways to grace and healing. Encouraging prayer, community involvement, and personal reflection are means by which individuals are led to redemption.

Moreover, this soul-searching isn't confined to those who have experienced abortion directly. It ripples through families, touching loved ones who might have supported the decision or remained silent. Each affected person embarks on their journey, seeking to untangle emotions and find peace. This shared quest for healing unites families and communities, prompting dialogue that, while difficult, is necessary for collective healing.

Through the tumult of emotions and the cloudy paths of doubt, the journey to healing and reconciliation is a testament to the human spirit's resilience. With each step forward, there's a deeper understanding that healing isn't a single destination but a lifelong pilgrimage. It calls for patience, openness, and an unwavering faith in the transformative power of love and forgiveness. And in this sacred journey, one gradually discovers how the fragmented pieces of their soul can be brought together, forming a tapestry of newfound hope and purpose.

The Role of the Church

In the midst of a society swayed by the relentless tides of modernity, where ethical debates often become mired in ambiguity, the Church stands as a steadfast beacon of moral clarity. Its voice, echoing from centuries of tradition and scriptural authority, assumes a critical role in navigating the spiritual consequences of abortion. The Church's teachings on the sanctity of life are not merely rituals of the old world; they are clarion calls to the conscience, asking believers to consider the profound spiritual dimensions of the choices they make.

For the Church, the issue of abortion transcends the realm of political discourse or scientific debate. It inhabits the sacred space of life itself, where every soul is viewed as a divine gift. The Church teaches that life begins at conception, and thus, abortion is seen as a grave violation of divine law. This perspective is rooted in the theological understanding that every human being, from the moment of conception, is imbued with a soul and dignity that demand recognition and protection.

The Church sees its role not merely as a guardian of doctrine but as a healer and guide for those grappling with the repercussions of abortion. Spiritual healing is offered through the sacraments, particularly Reconciliation, where individuals can seek forgiveness and find peace. This sacrament is not just a formality but a powerful encounter with God's mercy, enabling the faithful to heal the rift in their spiritual lives caused by abortion.

There is, however, a pastoral aspect that unfolds within the Church's mission. It is a commitment to accompanying individuals and families through their crises, offering support, counsel, and compassion without judgment. The Church encourages community-based support systems that foster an environment of care and understanding. These initiatives often extend beyond spiritual counsel, providing practical support to expectant mothers in need and advocating for policies that promote life and family welfare.

Moreover, the Church plays a significant role in education, imparting teachings that challenge societal norms and stimulate moral reflection. Through homilies, catechesis, and broader educational efforts, it aims to create an informed laity equipped to defend life. Education within the Church is not merely about passing knowledge but nurturing wisdom and discernment, allowing individuals to navigate complex moral landscapes with a well-formed conscience.

The teachings of the Church also extend to the global stage, engaging in dialogue with various cultures and governments to promote a universal ethic of life. The Church's presence in international forums and its advocacy for pro-life legislations highlight its commitment to influencing public policy and societal attitudes toward the dignity of human life. This dialogue is crucial in a world where relativism often obscures the intrinsic value of life.

In the social arena, the Church's role becomes even more pronounced in its critique of an "abortion culture" that reduces life to a commodity. Through encyclicals and public statements, the Church has consistently warned against a utilitarian mindset that places convenience above conscience. It urges society to seek solutions that uphold the dignity of all human beings, particularly the most vulnerable. GK Chesterton might have characterized this as a battle of ideas, where the paradox of freedom that enslaves rather than liberates demands a philosophical and ethical reckoning.

The Church also recognizes the importance of ecumenical and interfaith efforts in combating the abortion culture. Working alongside other religious traditions, it seeks common ground in the shared belief in the sanctity of human life. Such collaborations amplify the voice for life, transcending doctrinal differences to advocate for a civilization of love, rooted in a profound respect for life at all stages.

In a utopian vision, the Church sees a world where life is upheld as the most precious gift. However, it acknowledges the dystopian reality where life is often devalued or discarded. This dual recognition shapes its mission, grounding it in hope and realism. Pope Saint John Paul II, in his writings, envisioned a Culture of Life that transcends political ideologies and materialistic pursuits, urging believers to become witnesses of hope and participants in God's creation.

Ultimately, the role of the Church in this debate is not limited to advocacy or theological exposition. It embodies a call to conversion and transformation, inviting every soul to participate in the sacred mystery of life. In this invitation lies the Church's enduring relevance and its unwavering commitment to proclaiming the Gospel of Life. Through this witness, it seeks to bring healing and reconciliation, standing firmly as a moral compass in a world often adrift in ethical confusion.

Chapter 24: Women Who Reject Regret: Inspirational Stories

In a world that too often overlooks the quiet yet profound tales of resilience, the stories of women who have risen above the chains of regret speak volumes. These narratives are rich with courage and grace, illustrating how these women found a new path, embracing renewal and purpose amidst the aftermath of abortion. Their journeys defy the often one-dimensional portrayal of post-abortion experiences, revealing instead the textured landscape of hope and transformation. Drawing upon their inner strength, these women reconstruct their lives, building bridges between grief and grace. Their unwavering spirit shatters the myths perpetuated by an industry that promises freedom but often delivers heartache. Through personal accounts of strength and recovery, these women inspire a profound reflection on human dignity and the capacity for redemption. By sharing their stories, they not only empower others but illuminate a way forward where faith and forgiveness pave the road to healing. They are beacons demonstrating that beyond every shadow lies a resilient light, leading to a hopeful tomorrow.

Personal Accounts of Strength and Recovery

In the vast tapestry of human experience, few threads are as tangled with adversity and resilience as those woven by women who have faced the storms of regret and found the eye of recovery and strength. Their stories embody both the harrowing descent into despair and the remarkable ascent into hope. These narratives unfold not just as singular victories but as calls to a broader understanding of life, grace, and forgiveness.

Maria's journey began in the shadows of fear and uncertainty. She was young, facing a future that seemed ominously out of focus. Stumbling under the weight of expectation and pressure, she made a decision that was supposed to be liberating but instead became her deepest regret. For years, she wandered through a valley of guilt, her heart burdened with an abiding sorrow. It was through the gentle yet firm guidance of a faith-based community that Maria rediscovered her worth. Through every prayer and conversation, she felt the layers of regret peel away, revealing a strength she never knew she had. Faith became her beacon, illuminating her path out of darkness.

Then there's the tale of Claire, whose life spun off course following an abortion she wished she had never had. Her decision was made in a moment marred by external pressures and misinformation. Like many, she believed in the false assurances that this choice was harmless and easily reversible if need be. When the harsh reality set in, Claire found herself isolated, battling depression and anxiety. But it was within the arms of a supportive therapy group that she found solace and understanding. Listening to stories like hers, she began to piece together a new future, one that wasn't defined by past choices but by the potential for healing and growth.

The story of strength often follows the arc of forgiveness, not only from those around but from oneself. For Jasmine, forgiveness became a radical act of self-love. Her decision was entangled with a complex web of familial expectations and societal norms. The abortion left her feeling hollow and disconnected from the values she held dear. It was on a pilgrimage, while reflecting deeply on her spiritual path, that Jasmine realized grace was a gift she could give herself. Her recovery wasn't immediate but deliberate, each step forward fortified by prayer and contemplation on God's enduring mercy. Today, she teaches others about the power of faith in overcoming regret.

Samantha's experience diverges through the avenue of activism. Her abortion left her with a profound sense of loss that no platitudes could erase. She didn't want any other woman to feel the loneliness she endured. Determined to make a difference, she took her story to the public realm. Through speaking engagements and writing, she shared the raw truth of her journey. Her activism paved new roads to healing, allowing her to turn pain into purpose. In advocating for life, Samantha found her own voice and empowered others to listen to their own.

In an unexpected twist, Elena found redemption through reconciliation. Her decision was kept secret for years, a clandestine burden that kept her locked in emotional limbo. A chance meeting at a church conference opened a dialogue with a counselor who understood her plight. In open confession and with compassionate guidance, Elena confronted her past. The act of sharing her sorrow blossomed into a profound healing experience. Her strength grew not from her isolation but from her integration into a community that taught her the importance of vulnerability and shared humanity.

Each woman's journey reflects a unique tapestry of circumstances and resolutions, yet they are unified in their testament to the human spirit's capacity for renewal. These narratives do not negate the pain of their decisions; rather, they illustrate transformation through that pain. The ineffable strength found in faith, community, and self-acceptance often becomes the cornerstone upon which new lives are built.

The road from regret to recovery is rarely linear. It swerves and twists, testing resolve and patience. But within these trials exist opportunities for unparalleled growth. The women who have navigated this path serve as both beacons and mentors, reminding us that amidst profound suffering, hope can flourish. Their experiences lay bare the importance of understanding and compassion in a world too often devoid of these very qualities.

Alice, meanwhile, discovered the power of storytelling. After her abortion, she struggled with a profound sense of identity loss. She took to writing, not for others at first, but as a cathartic path to navigate her emotions. Through the written word, Alice confronted each regret, each pang of guilt. These writings, initially penned in solitude, eventually found an audience among those who shared her experiences. Her story resonated with others, allowing her not only to recover but to thrive by serving as a lighthouse for those still ensnared in the tempest of regret.

While not every story ends in triumph, every account offers vital lessons —lessons about human frailty, the boundless capacity for forgiveness, and the profound strength that emerges when one refuses to be shackled by regret. Across cultures and generations, these women's stories echo with a universal truth: redemption is not a single act, but a continuous journey towards grace, supported by a persistent belief in one's intrinsic worth.

In the broader narrative of abortion and its aftermath, these personal stories are not mere footnotes but foundational chapters that demand to be heard. They challenge facile narratives and invite a deeper contemplation of life's sanctity and the convoluted human journey. These accounts do more than recount individual resilience; they challenge society to reflect on choices, offer genuine alternatives, and extend unwavering support and love to those seeking redemption amidst their regrets.

By sharing these stories and amplifying these voices, we not only honor the women who have walked this path but also empower future generations to choose life, informed with wisdom and encouraged by hope. As these narratives of recovery continue to inspire, they remind us all that from the depths of regret, strength can indeed emerge, and with it, a life reclaimed and remade.

Building a Life After Abortion

In the delicate aftermath of an abortion, life has to be rebuilt, often with painstaking care and courage. The physical procedures and emotional tumult may leave scars, but the resilience of the human spirit shines as an indomitable force. Women who face the daunting task of rebuilding their lives after such an experience find unique challenges and opportunities waiting for them at every turn. Their stories serve as universal testaments to human strength, illuminating paths to growth, healing, and profound transformation.

For many, the journey begins with a quiet introspection, a need to understand the profound changes that have occurred within themselves. This introspection is not just about coming to terms with the past but also about redefining one's own identity and the future that lies ahead. It's about confronting and dispelling the societal myths that linger around abortion —myths that paint women with broad strokes of regret and sorrow.

The path of rebuilding life requires an acknowledgment of the emotional landscape that comes after abortion. Many women experience a range of emotions, from grief and loss to relief and empowerment. Each woman's journey is deeply personal, navigating through this tumultuous sea of feelings towards a shore of clarity and purpose. As they delve deeper into their own experiences, some women find solace in the narratives shared by others who have walked the same path, illustrating the shared human ordeal of rebirth.

One of the most compelling aspects of these stories is the role of forgiveness—both self-forgiveness and the forgiveness of others. In a world quick to judge, the act of forgiving oneself can be a radical journey of self-acceptance and love. It is this forgiveness that can act as a catalyst, allowing women to shed the layers of guilt imposed upon them by external forces and their own inner doubts.

As these women work to forgive themselves, they often encounter communities ready to offer support. Faith-based organizations, counseling groups, and community networks play a pivotal role in providing resources and safe spaces for healing. Compassionate guidance and unwavering support from loved ones and community groups can make the difference between stumbling alone and walking together through the pain.

Many women find themselves compelled to emerge from the shadow of their experience, inspired to make a difference for others. They contribute by sharing their stories, volunteering, or leading initiatives that provide hope and support for pregnant women facing similar choices. Determined to prevent others from experiencing the same anguish, they engage in advocacy and education, empowering women with knowledge and options beyond abortion.

Each story of recovery and reconstruction is a powerful narrative of hope —not just for them individually but for the society as a whole. These women's paths of recovery remind us of the innate strength every individual possesses. They illustrate that it's indeed possible to traverse the darkest of times and emerge with renewed purpose, redefining one's life beyond the confines of regret.

Moreover, an essential component of this recovery often involves revisiting one's spiritual beliefs. For many, the Church stands as a beacon of hope and a source of strength and direction. Engaging in spiritual practices or finding community within the Church can facilitate a reconnection with one's faith. It's in these moments of spiritual solace that many women find the courage to embrace forgiveness truly, not only looking at their own lives through a compassionate lens but also encouraging a broader societal conversation about the moral intricacies involved.

As women build lives post-abortion, they often become torchbearers of change, illuminating paths for others who might otherwise feel lost in the abyss of their choices. By sharing their journeys, they help dismantle misconceptions, offering alternative narratives filled with resilience, understanding, and grace.

In essence, "Building a Life After Abortion" transcends the boundaries of personal healing to touch upon the broader themes of societal transformation and collective empathy. It is a call to action for society to approach the subject of abortion not with haste and judgment but with a profound understanding of the human condition and the complexities of individual stories.

Through these rebuilt lives, we are reminded of the potential for growth after adversity. It emphasizes the crucial importance of support systems, love, and understanding in navigating the complexities of life after abortion. These are not merely stories of overcoming; they are narratives of thriving beyond the shadows, driven by resilience and guided by a vision for a more compassionate world.

Chapter 25: The Unseen Costs of Abortion to Humanity

In a world where moral fibers are continuously tested, the unseen costs of abortion stretch beyond individual experiences to permeate the very core of our society. As we navigate through this dense forest of existential dilemmas, abortion quietly chips away at the bedrock of human values, redefining what it means to cherish life. The process subtly desensitizes societies, causing a shift in how future generations comprehend dignity and the sanctity of life. Like a single thread unraveling a tapestry, abortion's societal implications threaten to mar the intricate weave of human connection and compassion. The gravity of this shift is illuminated not merely in statistics, but more hauntingly, in the eroding empathy evident across cultures and faiths. Ultimately, this chapter asks us to reconsider the trajectory of humanity's moral compass, questioning if the path paved by abortion leads to a utopia of autonomy or a dystopia where life's sacredness is a relic of the past.

Societal Desensitization

In the quiet corridors of society, where values are shaped and norms are as soft as clay, something profound and unsettling has taken root. The pervasive nature of abortion practices, quietly endorsed, or sometimes vehemently defended, has affected our collective perception of life's sanctity. A slow, almost imperceptible numbing of sensitivity towards the beginnings of life is making its subtle yet impactful way into the DNA of human consciousness.

Imagine a world where the value of a human being is debated not on the basis of intrinsic worth but on arbitrary criteria such as convenience, economic standing, or societal impact. With each whispered acceptance of abortion, society edges closer to an abyss where the miraculous process of life is reduced to a mere checklist of characteristics and conditions. Herein lies the danger—the gradual erosion of compassion that once held human life as sacred above all else.

It's not just the repeated statistics and clinical terminology that contribute to this desensitization. It's the way these narratives are woven through various aspects of modern culture—the media, literature, and political rhetoric. This saturation has made it easy for society to default to a more utilitarian view of existence, where discussions about potential life are dominated by factors other than moral philosophy or ethical considerations.

The shift is reminiscent of historical epochs where dehumanization began with language, often subtly. Once words that described the unborn were rooted in a future of promise and potential. They have since transformed into sterile, mechanical descriptors. This shift linguistically distances us from the emotional and spiritual connections that should ideally gird our treatment and understanding of all stages of life.

A pertinent consequence of this desensitization is the impact on how society perceives ethical quandaries at large. As the line blurs between what is morally sound and what is socially acceptable, the foundational pillars of communities risk crumbling. This allows for more ethically dubious practices to gain acceptance, simply due to familiarity breeding complicity among the populace.

Parents are left in a conundrum about instilling values in their children, causing them to question if they're preparing their offspring for a world that has redefined right and wrong. The family unit, one of the last bastions of unconditional love and life-centered nurturing, finds itself on shaky ground. Discussions around life's inception become dichotomous battles rather than reflections of deep societal unity.

However, this trend is not without historical parallels. As societies slip into complacency regarding once-contested moral issues, they often awaken to find themselves on the brink of crises that threaten their core integrity. History shows us that without reflection or resistance, many communities have found moral decline to be only a precursor to broader destabilization, politically and socially.

Yet, in the midst of this challenge lies a unique opportunity. The very nature of desensitization means that the human spirit has an unquestionable capacity to rehumanize what seems lost. By rekindling conversations centered on empathy, community, and the recognition of life's inherent value, society can break free from this cycle of numbness.

It's worth considering what role education might have in this process. If future generations are taught to appreciate life not just for its potentials and possibilities, but for its essence, society might find its equilibrium once again. Educational curricula rooted in philosophy, ethics, and reflective discourse could serve as catalysts for renewing societal sensitivity.

Faith-based organizations and spiritual leaders might also play a critical role in restoring some of this desensitization. With a stance that transcends political or cultural divides, they hold the potential to unify and reorient discussions around life, using compassion and understanding as guiding forces.

The rehumanization journey could also draw strength from literature and the arts, realms that have historically acted as mirrors to society's best and worst inclinations. By depicting the sanctity of life with clarity and nuance, art can draw individuals into more profound personal reflections, springboarding societal change.

We must reject complacency and embrace a mindset that continually seeks to question, understand and recalibrate what it means to hold life in the highest esteem. This means addressing not only the personal choices but also societal structures that obscure the gravity of these decisions. It means advocating for policies that emphasize life-supporting alternatives, equipping individuals with the resources and knowledge to make values-driven decisions.

The possibility of societal desensitization is a clarion call—one that demands introspection and, most importantly, action. Recognizing its existence is the first step, with the subsequent challenge being to foster an environment where life, in all its forms, is celebrated and protected. This is not merely a moral imperative but a societal necessity, one with the potential to reforge our collective identity with compassion and grace.

As we consider the implications of our current path, let us summon wisdom from the past and hope for the future. In doing so, we might just find that the seeds of societal desensitization can be replaced by ones of empathy, resilience, and renewed commitment to the sanctity of life. Through concerted effort and a willingness to alter the status quo, the unseen costs to humanity can transform into visible gains for generations yet to come.

Long-Term Impact on Human Values

In the vast tapestry of human values, few threads have been as subtly disrupted as those touched by the implications of abortion. It is a practice that has quietly woven its way into the social fabric, often challenging the core tenets that underpin our collective moral and ethical compass. Over time, as laws and norms around abortion shifted, a recalibration of values occurred, one that questions the fundamental respect for life and what it means to embrace the sanctity of existence from its earliest stages.

To understand the long-term impact of abortion on human values, we must first recognize the profound influence it exerts on concepts of life and human dignity. For centuries, many cultures grounded their moral systems on the inviolability of human life. This foundational belief shaped laws, ethics, and religions. With the advent and normalization of abortion, however, came a gradual erosion of this value, where the definition of "when life begins" became not just a philosophical inquiry but an issue subject to legal interpretations and personal beliefs.

More than just a societal practice, abortion has challenged our perception of responsibility and reverence for life itself. It poses difficult questions: Are we the arbiters of life and death? How do we balance personal autonomy with moral responsibility? Historically, these have been profound ethical inquiries faced by humanity, often guided by tradition and belief. The precedence of choice in the context of abortion risks diminishing the perceived value of life, fundamentally altering how society approaches decisions impacting future generations.

Furthermore, as abortion became more widespread, the ethical discussions surrounding it shifted, often becoming more technical and clinical. This shift represented not only a detachment from the metaphysical and spiritual dimensions of life but also a means to dehumanize what was once considered sacred. Over time, what was a deeply moral dilemma about life transformed into a discourse dominated by rights and liberties, minimizing the broader dialogue about moral duty and collective human conscience.

One must also consider the implications of abortion on familial and societal constructs. The very essence of family as a nurturing and life-affirming institution faces challenges when the value of a potential life is weighed against personal or economic convenience. Within a family, each member plays a critical role; the potential loss of any member, even one unborn, alters the dynamic. Families and communities, which historically provided the bedrock for moral lessons, find themselves navigating complex ethical landscapes where individual choice sometimes challenges communal values.

Moreover, legal systems around the world have had to grapple with these evolving values. Laws are not merely rules that regulate behavior; they are reflections of the values that society collectively upholds. As abortion gained legislative backing in many parts of the world, it further signaled a shift in value systems, prioritizing autonomy over age-old collective moral imperatives. This legal endorsement implicitly questions prior moral stances, suggesting a shift in ethical priorities.

The subtle, yet profound impact on education is also noteworthy. As future generations are raised within contexts where abortion is a legal and commonly discussed option, it informs their understanding of human life from a young age. The moral teachings that once emphasized the giftedness of life and the consequences of its termination now must contend with narratives that often normalize the choice of abortion.

Can society sustain itself on a moral foundation that increasingly leans towards individual rights at the perceived expense of communal ethics? The question reverberates through communities, echoing in schools, churches, and families. It's a question without an easy answer, yet its presence beckons a reinvestment in understanding and potentially redefining values that have guided humanity for centuries.

From a spiritual perspective, the long-term impact of abortion challenges the divine vision of life as a blessing. Many faith traditions underscore the belief that life begins at conception, a sacred gift from the Creator. Each aborted life, therefore, represents not just physical loss, but a spiritual void, an opportunity missed for potential to blossom into reality, whether in joy, challenge, or triumph.

Despite these challenges, the human spirit remains resilient, continually re-evaluating and redefining its values in the face of new realities. Communities across the world have embarked on dialogues seeking to harmonize new liberties with age-old moral imperatives. Faith-based initiatives strive to bridge the gap between emerging rights and traditional values, offering hope and reconciliation.

The task ahead requires courage and wisdom, involving a dialogue that embraces complexity yet seeks clarity. It necessitates an honest exploration of what it means to live in a society where human values evolve, but where core moral pillars need affirmation and defense. By recognizing these shifts and impacts, society has the potential to reaffirm its commitment to uphold human dignity, grounded in compassion and guided by the wisdom of both past and present.

As we ponder the enduring effects of these changes, it becomes apparent that what is at stake is more than individual choices or societal norms— it's the very heart of what it means to be human. The ongoing discourse about abortion and its moral dimensions challenges us not just to react but to reason deeply, to hold steadfastly to values that define the collective conscience, and to inspire future generations to understand the profound significance of life's sacredness.

Conclusion

The journey through the complex and multifaceted world of abortion has been both enlightening and sobering. It's a path lined with controversies, deeply personal experiences, and significant societal implications. We've delved into medical procedures, the underpinnings of politics and economy, and the profound impact on individuals and their families. This exploration reveals abortion not as a mere medical procedure, but as a pivot point around which many critical moral and ethical discussions revolve.

Abortion is more than a choice; it is a reflection of societal values and principles. Each chapter in this work has peeled back layers that often remain unexamined in public discourse. From exploring hidden agendas within the abortion industry to the ethical conundrum faced by medical practitioners, it's evident that the issue is deeply seated in moral challenges that stretch across time and culture. It compels us to question where we stand as a society on the value of life and human dignity.

The impact of abortion stretches beyond individual narratives. It reaches into the collective consciousness, influencing societal norms and future generations. The economic ramifications are significant, but the moral and spiritual costs are perhaps the most profound. As a society, nurturing the human spirit demands a reevaluation of how we approach life and death, choice and responsibility. The silent cries of regret and the whispers of loss paint a dystopian landscape that beckons for healing and understanding.

A recurring theme throughout this examination has been the tension between pro-life and pro-choice ideologies. The divisive nature of this debate often overshadows the fundamental questions of human rights and dignity. In seeking to resolve this tension, we must move beyond argument and rhetoric to embrace a dialogue that acknowledges the fears, hopes, and dreams of all involved. Finding common ground requires empathy, humility, and the courage to challenge preconceived notions.

The voices of those who've walked the path of abortion — whether in regret or resilience — tell stories that demand recognition and reflection. These personal accounts offer a window into the complex emotional landscape post-abortion and highlight the need for robust support systems. We can't underestimate the power of community, faith, and education in nurturing recovery and providing a lifeline to those who seek it. Their stories compel us to strengthen these networks and enhance supportive measures for women and families.

As we look to the future, the intersection of legal battles and scientific advancements poses new ethical questions. Legislation will continue to evolve, influenced by court decisions and societal shifts, but it must be grounded in a commitment to uphold human life and rights. As technology progresses, how we perceive life and its inception must remain anchored in ethical considerations that honor both science and morality. It is imperative that these advancements serve humanity, elevating rather than dehumanizing us.

The conclusion comes not as an end, but as a call to action. It challenges us to reconsider how we as individuals, communities, and societies respond to the myriad aspects of abortion. It urges us towards advocacy grounded in truth and compassion, education that enlightens, and policies that protect the most vulnerable. Above all, it beckons us to reaffirm the sanctity of life as a cornerstone of our shared human experience.

In the final assessment, ending abortion's tragic legacy requires concerted efforts across moral, social, and legal dimensions. It's a vision not just for a future free of the pain and division wrought by this issue, but for a world where every life is cherished, every heart can heal, and every soul finds its place in the embrace of humanity. This is not mere idealism; it is the promise within reach if we commit to shaping a world grounded in hope, justice, and love.

Appendix A: Resources for Further Information

To fully understand the complexities surrounding the issue of abortion, it is crucial to delve into an array of resources that offer diverse perspectives and insights. This appendix provides a guide to resources that can further inform and deepen your understanding, particularly from the viewpoint of Roman Catholics, historians, and expectant mothers.

Books and Literature

- ***Evangelium Vitae*** by Pope John Paul II - A profound encyclical addressing the value and inviolability of human life.
- ***Abortion and the Conscience of the Nation*** by Ronald Reagan - Offers perspective on the moral implications of abortion.
- ***Love and Responsibility*** by Karol Wojtyla (Pope John Paul II) - Explores human ethics, sexuality, and responsibility from a Catholic viewpoint.

Documentaries and Films

- ***The Silent Scream*** - A documentary that presents the process of abortion through ultrasound imagery.
- ***Unplanned*** - A film based on the true story of a former Planned Parenthood director who became a pro-life advocate.

Scientific and Medical Journals

- *Journal of Medical Ethics* - Features articles exploring the ethical dimensions of abortion.
- *New England Journal of Medicine* - Includes studies and papers on the impacts and methods related to abortion.

Online Resources and Organizations

- United States Conference of Catholic Bishops - Provides resources and statements on pro-life activities and teachings.
- Human Life International - Offers articles and advocacy resources promoting a culture of life.
- Feminists for Life - An organization that presents a pro-life feminist perspective.

Experiential and Support Networks

- ***Project Rachel*** - A healing ministry for those who seek reconciliation and healing after abortion.
- ***Rachel's Vineyard*** - Provides retreats aimed at spiritual and emotional healing for women and men.
- ***Option Line*** - An organization that connects individuals to pregnancy help centers across the United States.

Each of these resources offers unique insights and knowledge. They serve as a pivotal step toward a more informed and compassionate perspective on the issues surrounding abortion, encouraging a dialogue rooted in understanding, empathy, and ethical reflection.

www.ingramcontent.com/pod-product-compliance
Lightning Source LLC
Chambersburg PA
CBHW060114120726
48003CB00009B/2637